EDUCATING FOOTBALL

STEVE SALLIS

EDUCATING FOOTBALL

Steve Sallis © 2024
www.solutionsmindset.com

ISBN 978-1-912009-08-4

First Published in 2018 by Compass-Publishing
www.compass-publishing.com

Printed in the United Kingdom by CMP Group Ltd

A catalogue version of the book can be found at the British Library

Designed and edited by The Book Refinery Ltd
www.thebookrefinery.com

Cover Photo by Tony Gameiro
About the Author photo by Scott Parry Photography

All rights reserved. No part of this publication may be reproduced or distributed in any form or by any means, or stored in a data base or retrieval system, without the prior written permission of the author.

Dedication

This book is dedicated to all my readers, friends, family, parents and teachers. It's also for the coaches who care about our footballing future and educational evolution.

CONTENTS

FOREWORD *by Jimmy Bullard, Dave Livermore and Paul Stretch* 9
A NOTE FROM THE AUTHOR..13
INTRODUCTION 17

SECTION ONE: WARM UP – FOOTBALL FOUNDATIONS - 23

Chapter 1 - Football Irony: Bullard the Manager 25
Chapter 2 - Talent: The Most Overused Word in Sport.................................31
Chapter 3 - Winners! How do you Create Them?..35
Chapter 4 - How to Achieve Success: A Young Athlete's Approach..............43
Chapter 5 - The Mario Balotelli Effect and 'Difficult' Footballers 47
Chapter 6 - The 10,000 Hours of Practice Rule! 53
Chapter 7 - What is Development in Football for Youth Athletes?...............59
Chapter 8 - 3 Point Football: Performance Where it Counts 65

SECTION TWO: FIRST HALF – TEACHING TIPS - 71

Chapter 9 - Seven Million is too Many! 73
Chapter 10 - What is Knowledge and Learning for Elite Coaches
and Teachers?..79
Chapter 11 - The Problem With Teachers 85
Chapter 12 - The Importance of 'Adding Value' in Sport..............................89

CONTENTS

Chapter 13 - 'Accelerated Learning' and What it Really Means in Football .97

Chapter 14 - The Power and Problem of Performance Data and the C/D Borderline Players 103

SECTION THREE: HALF TIME – COACHING CHAMPIONS - 109

Chapter 15 - The Singer Not the Song 111

Chapter 16 - The Maverick Coach 115

Chapter 17 - "He Can't Do That!" The Coach Mindset Phenomenon 121

Chapter 18 - Teacher or Coach? What Are You? Are Coaches Missing a Trick? 127

Chapter 19 - Stop Interrupting! Let Them Finish 131

Chapter 20 - The Half-Time Team Talk: Time to be a Teacher! 135

Chapter 21 - Leadership in Sport 141

Chapter 22 - Football Philosophy: The Prizes and the Pitfalls 149

Chapter 23 - Follow the Process … and you get Progress 153

SECTION FOUR: SECOND HALF – TEAMWORK TRAINING - 159

Chapter 24 - The Importance of TEAMwork! 161

Chapter 25 - No Dickheads! The Importance of Group Dynamics for Success in TEAMS 169

Chapter 26 - Sports Teams: IMPROVE them or REPLACE them? 173

Chapter 27 - Behaviour Management or Behaviour for Learning? 179

Chapter 28 - Elite Athletes and Resilience... Born, Made or Destroyed? ...193

Chapter 29 - Sport Psychology: What is it?..201

SECTION FIVE THE FINAL WHISTLE:
THE POWER OF PARENTS – GOOD AND BAD - 211

Chapter 30 - The Secret Parents: Trials and Tribulations.........................213

Chapter 31 The Wrong Type of Love and Parent Envy:
How to Hinder Your Children 229

SECTION SIX: EXTRA TIME – THE EXTRAS - 233

Chapter 32 - The Secret Footballer: Life After Football..............................235

Chapter 33 - The Story of True Resilience: Our Journey *by Ebere Eze* 239

Chapter 34 - "Sports Science Appliance" 243

Chapter 35 - The Theory of Luck in Football! 249

Chapter 36 - Insecure PERSON multiplied by Incompetent PERSON
= DANGEROUS PERSON...255

Chapter 37 - "It's OK not to be OK" 259

Chapter 38 - The Death of Dialogue 263

Chapter 39 - 10 Tips for 'Emotional Intelligence' in Sport and
Why it's Number One for SUCCESS!..267

CONCLUSION 273

ABOUT THE AUTHOR..277

ACKNOWLEDGEMENTS..279

FOREWORD

BY JIMMY BULLARD, DAVE LIVERMORE AND PAUL STRETCH

Jimmy Bullard – Former Wigan, Fulham and Hull City Professional

In simple terms, I chose Steve Sallis to become my assistant manager. I had several options, hundreds in fact, but it was obvious he was the stand out candidate. His professional experiences are off the charts and his understanding of how people operate and think is the best I have ever witnessed. When Steve speaks, people listen. He has that way. You can't coach that. His preparation is meticulous. His way with players is first class and his knowledge of the game unbelievable. He was good for me; always calm, but with a winning mentality. We taught each other, but he taught me things I'll carry into management forever. What a guy.

David Livermore – Ex Professional Footballer and Millwall FC Assistant Manager and Pro License Holder

If you asked me to describe my relationship with Steve Sallis in a handful of words, I would certainly fail at picking the right ones. It's simply impossible to capture him so succinctly. I have known him for five years and I still cannot think of a single adjective that can fully describe all that he is. As his work colleague, I have seen him as a hardworking and committed man. In fact, we started out as work colleagues and quickly upgraded each other to friends. As a friend, Steve is supportive, caring and thoughtful, but he also isn't afraid to disagree with you. Instead of feeding you answers, he will give you a shot of honesty and leave you to think about it. That is the real strength of Steve's personality.

If you are reading this book to find definitive answers, you are in for a surprise. That is simply not Steve's way, either as a friend or as an educator. This book is bound to leave you with more questions than answers, but it will also inspire curiosity. Steve Sallis is not always the man who gives you the right answers; he is the man who makes you ask all the right questions.

He is the one who makes you reflect until you reach the right conclusion. If I had a pound for all the times Steve challenged me, disagreed with me or openly questioned the 'customary' way of doing things, I would be a millionaire. This, in essence, is what makes Steve so helpful. He will always give you the other perspective so you can weigh your views against it, even though it might result in debates that border on an argument, but also make you more thoughtful and critical. These skills are indispensable to someone working in a field as dynamic as professional football. Steve raised the bar when he entered our building. Those players need to feel grateful; in the elite environment, this man is cutting edge.

"How do you know if you don't know, right?" is a question you will hear Steve ask all too often. Now that I'm thinking about it, these words are profound. They encourage you to test things out and see for yourself what suits you. On the topic of player learning and development, Steve's opinions will often completely clash with those of other people, as well as my own. He is unapologetic when he makes a case for them. This keeps us all from rushing into decisions without considering the alternatives. We all benefit from Steve's way and now pause before making important decisions and consider all the possible solutions and alternatives. Doing this has helped me broaden my knowledge and learn more in both a personal as well as a professional capacity.

Steve speaks to you through this book as a friend, and he will do for you what he does for me. He will help you understand why you think the way you think, and how your personal experiences shape you. He will also help you break down the barriers you create for yourself by shutting yourself away inside your comfort zone. At certain points you will find this book challenging, at others you will find yourself reflecting. It would be dishonest of me to claim that this book contains all there is to know about teaching, coaching, leadership, parenting, and more – no book can do that – but I can assure you that it will make you realise that learning is an ongoing process and a lifelong commitment. By asking the right questions, you can continue to nurture yourself and those around you.

Paul Stretch - Lead Physical Preparation Coach – Men's Senior Great Britain and England Hockey

Having spent a decade in elite sport, Steve has, without question, had the greatest influence on me as a professional. He is a constant source of inspiration to his peers, players and all those associated with the organisations he works for.

Steve has an outstanding technical knowledge about human behaviour, which he communicates with clarity and consistency. I have witnessed first-hand his ability to initiate change in players' attitudes and inspire innovation. He is a genuinely impactful individual who can transform even the toughest environments into ones that breed learning and creativity.

A NOTE FROM THE AUTHOR

So, on January 31st 2021, I received a phone call. From Mark Robinson. "Sallis, I'm going to need your help," he said.

"What with?" I replied.

"I'm the new Head Coach of AFC Wimbledon, the greatest story in English Football, and I want to know if you're in? Do you want to be my new Head of Performance Mindset?" he asked.

So, this was it! Time to apply what I have written about in this book and see if it works. At first-team level. And it did!

We joined the club in the bottom four of the league table in League 1 (England's third tier), when the team had only won one game in the last 11. We finished the season in the top 10 in the form table, and six places higher than when we began.

The ppg (points per game) before we joined was 0.91

End of season it was 1.11 . . .

That really is adding value . . . by a whopping 21.2%. Any business CEO would rate that wouldn't they? We relegated big name managers like Joey Barton and John Sheriden respectively. And our backroom staff of 'unknown underdogs' did the job we set out to accomplish.

Our backroom team of myself, Mark Robinson, Rob Tuvey, Ashley Bayes, Justin Cochrane, Andy Parslow, James Oliver Pearce, Goncalo Pinto, Tim Maynard, Chris McConnell, Vicky Newbold, Katy Bignell, Robin Bedford, Geoff, and Trevor. What people you are! It's been a pleasure working with you. We did it. We created history.

28th March 2022

Afc Wimbledon announce the sacking of the brilliant Robbo. Yes you heard it. He was brilliant and still got the boot. The easiest way to describe our success:

- We were 5th bottom of the league last season with a player Joe Pigott that had scored 24 goals.
- This year, we were 5th bottom; without Joe Pigott who had never been replaced. (Note sarcasm)
- The average of the team reduced from 28 to 22 in 12 months. One player Ayoub Assal called into the England U20 squad, and
- The youngest squad in the Football League.
- Yes we were in relegation. But we were last year and got out of it. I backed us to do the same. The supporters led board clearly didn't.

It's now 11th April 2022 and I am still waiting for someone from the board to call me. Yes, ridiculous I appreciate. And we wonder why football has a bad name!

The good news however was on Saturday 13th November 2021 an old colleague from Millwall Fc Steve Morison (Morro) was placed in charge at Cardiff City. We speak on the phone and he wants me in to help him, the staff and the team stay clear of relegation after many games without a win under the previous manager Mick McCarthy. As the clubs are in two different leagues there is no conflict of interest so I accept the offer.

I call Morro the "iceman". He is zero bullshit. He has no grey areas in his methodology apart from on his pristine haircut. As a player he was a no-nonsense centre forward, leader and had much success on the pitch. He has huge presence physically, standing at 6ft 2 inches. But his persona is calm and calculated. He says very little. Stands back and observes, but when he does speak people listen. That's a rarity and art form. I'm still telling to him smile more on camera but that will come. Dealing with press isn't easy.

He is clever as he knows his super strengths, and knows his area of weakness. This high level of self-awareness early in his managerial career is going to hold him in good stead of course. I've said many times, *"An expert hires an expert."* His backroom staff include the articulate Mark Hudson, the diligent Tom Ramasut and both are the ideal foils for Morro. Andy Dibble the GK coach is caring and loyal to his keepers.

Mark had great career, captaining most clubs he played for and you can see why. A true gentleman and professional human being. Tom, a little like me had a youth career in pro football, but went into coaching early in his life and has been at Cardiff for many years coaching, and learning his trade in teaching and learning at the clubs Academy.

I'm in the club on an ad-hoc basis to simply add value in my way, but also look at the longer term strategy of the process, than the typical "knee jerk" football bullshit that happens at most clubs. These diverse experiences provide a perfect mix of skills for any backroom team. After all, "Everybody knows more than somebody".

Morro secured the Manager of the Month for March 2022 and his tenure has seen a steady increase in points per game from 0.8 to 1.5. Double the output with the same group of players. Who says strategists don't matter?

Sunday 18th September 2022

Steve Morison gets sacked. The ultimate guarantee in professional football is being sacked. He kept the team in the league the previous season and his reward is to be sacked. Complete nonsense after bringing in 15 new players and cutting the wage bill by 50%. These owners really do need self-awareness training. It also means I am gone.

Monday 19th September 2022

The phone rings. It's Jon Brady, the Northampton Town manager. "Sallis what are you doing on Thursday? Can you give me some help?" So, after helping two teams avoid relegation, it's now my time to go for a promotion charge in League 2. Watch this space.

Sunday May 8th 2023

Tranmere 0-1 Northampton

We're promoted after a gruelling 46 game season. Jon Brady is a hero. Colin Calderwood the ultimate voice of reason, and me just tidying up the process for all.

Football strategy now wins for three seasons on the bounce.

INTRODUCTION

This book is the result of a 22-year journey, from a failed footballer turned teacher in PE and assistant headteacher, to the Head of Education and Player Welfare, and part of Millwall Football Club Academy's management team, to, finally, a business founder. I wrote this book for many reasons. Why? Because although the football industry has made some great strides forward over the last decade, I still believe it has a long, long way to go in terms of employing the word 'professional' accurately. Let's be honest here; although the industry is improving, many institutionalised people are still involved in it. Mostly they only know about football and they often aren't aware that they 'don't know what they don't know'. You see, knowing about football isn't enough and I don't think it ever has been. After all, what is the point of knowing about football if you don't know about people, psychology, emotional intelligence, teaching, truly effective learning or even leadership? You must know that football has been my life, but so has education. I therefore feel it is only right for me to share with you what I have seen, heard and experienced regarding human capability in both sporting and non-sporting environments, and how the two correlate in order to achieve greatness and help people help others to become better at their job. It is important to remember that Gerrard Houllier, Paul Clement, Arsene Wenger, Louis Van Gaal, Rinus Michels, Guss Hiddink, Roy Hodgson and, of course, the Cowley brothers were all teachers. That's not a bad list, I suppose!

Without my rollercoaster educational experiences, which started when, as a new secondary student, I was placed in the bottom set in 1988 and subsequently set up to fail all of my GCSEs in the summer of 1993, only to retake them, scrape a few A Levels and get a degree, become a teacher and, subsequently, a university lecturer and find my true purpose, I wouldn't have been able to make an impact in the football industry. You see, my journey has been tough and failures have happened everywhere, but my passion for 'learning about learning' is never-ending. In addition, having a firm grasp of sporting education, teaching knowledge, learning, coaching, rewards, sanctions, motivation, emotional intelligence and the strategic and operational demands of youth development requires experience. I have two decades' experience in education and sport, which makes me understand it in a greater depth than I could ever have imagined when I started my journey as an aspiring professional footballer at Brighton and Hove Albion or as a trainee teacher.

This book will help you quickly evaluate your life map and your journey, so that you will further understand that your reality and experiences in life around teaching, coaching, leading or parenting are not the same as everyone else's. You will understand the importance of 'zooming out' more often than you 'zoom in' and appreciate to a greater level how this mindset is a vital ingredient of any so-called expert. But this book is bigger than just football; it will challenge you to gain a better understanding of self-awareness, teaching, learning, leadership, psychology, team culture, high-end performance, youth development, behavioural strategies and how strategic and operational concepts help to make development easier for people of all ages.

Why?

What I have learnt and what you will learn from reading this book is that you are basically stuffed if you lack self-awareness, because having self-awareness is the beginning of the development journey that will lead to a better life. The know-it-alls may well be right, but we often know they are wrong. The England national football team played a rigid 4-4-2 formation for decades. The experts choosing this process were clearly not challenged, or perhaps didn't want to be. But for whatever reason, we were sent down the wrong path with our players. I have always said that if footballers like Rio Ferdinand were Italian, they would have played regularly for their country from the age of 17 and acquired 150 caps. Instead, England waited until he was 21 before allowing him to play regularly. It's a little like the schooling system, I suppose. We know that in years to come some of the processes going on now will be viewed as majorly flawed, but no one is willing to be brave enough to change them now. The exam factory culture is causing mayhem in schools and people's home life. You see, people development is about people and not always about a laptop, smartphone or bit of technology. It is about human interaction and the energy you feel around people. You only have to be in or around a football changing room or a successful school or business to see this. My 'why' for writing this book and my 'why' for helping people is simple. I love it! Those who know me are aware that I am an emotional guy. I care about stuff ... people, society, communities and beyond. I have cried after leaving every school I have ever worked in. When I left Blackheath Bluecoat School in 2012 after a nine-year stint and received a standing ovation from 1000 kids and 100 teachers, I got more than a bit teary. Trust me, this stuff makes you emotional.

So, my passion for people development simply gives me my 'why'. I love the energy and emotion it provides. Being involved in professional football has helped me realise that this is my true place in life. This is where I belong. And as I write this, I am proud to say that 10 months into my business, people from all walks of life are requesting my expertise. I have spoken at England's HQ, St George's Park, as a key note speaker, supported headteachers across the country with my resilience and wellbeing project and provided leadership training for city professionals. In addition, I have taught professional athletes about mental conditioning and given them performance support and I have coached and mentored various people and taught teachers at all stages of their career. That's what I do and that's who I am. My advice? Be you, but be the best version of you.

Additionally, I suppose I feel I was let down by the system from childhood. At 11 it labelled me below intelligent. Five years later, I was dubbed stupid for not getting any GCSEs. In 1993, I was seen by society as thick because I'd achieved no A-C grade passes, but a year later I was called brainy for retaking my exams and gaining seven. I mean, really?

The facts: I had parents that pushed me to go again while juggling playing football. Plus, feeling like I had massively let myself down made me more mature. You see, failure made me write this book. It is my fuel and gives me my drive to prove to society and beyond that providing you have the right support and people around you, anything is possible.

How is understanding this concept going to make you a better coach?

All top coaches know that knowing about 11v11 isn't enough to be the best as a coach or leader. This book will challenge you by providing as many questions as it does answers. It will help you whether you are a Sunday league junior coach or a high performing elite coach. What I learnt by coming into the football industry from a background in education was that in terms of strategy, football was far behind. Basically, there often wasn't any. The gap is closing for sure, and the coaching industry has finally upped its game with high-end teaching, learning and strategic methodology, which is being used effectively on coaching licenses and in clubs.

What this book is not

It isn't a magic wand, it doesn't have all the answers – but it will make you think differently about who you are and how you operate.

How to read this book

This book probably isn't one to read from front to back. Some chapters will appeal much more than others so select ones to read that you feel are necessary; the book has been carefully arranged to facilitate this. From my understanding, many people are busy these days and don't read very often. This isn't because they don't want to, but because they don't have the time. I have deliberately created chapters that should take you no more than five to 15 minutes to read. I advise you to have an open mind and to challenge yourself about why I am saying the things I do.

You will sometimes read a chapter and not initially understand my concepts. That's OK, because my advice about learning is clear and calm, and the need to revisit learning in life is key. Rereading chapters will be necessary on occasion, as learning isn't always clean.

As I mentioned, I am very calm about this book prompting as many questions as it provides answers. This is simply because I do not claim to have all the answers. In some sections, I don't hold back about some of the poor practices I have witnessed on my journey. To be able to give advice and help people improve themselves and those around them is a passion of mine. But if you are involved in sport or development at any level, from amateur to elite, it can and will help you if you let it.

> *I want you to truly understand that 'self awareness' is the key driver to human change and personal growth.*

Without self awareness:

- You have no hope. You become unconsciously incompetent.
- You are unable to develop, improve and truly understand where you and your knowledge are at, which will prevent you from moving forwards.

My professor for my Masters degree, Dr Bob Burstow, simply enabled me to access a new level of learning that I didn't see as available at the time. He gave me access to knowledge I knew nothing about. But mostly, Bob taught me the meaning of true intelligence and that being wise, professional and kind are by far the best ways to influence people (rather than using fear and autocracy). He also enabled me to access meta-cognition – and this word has simply changed my life. I won't tell you what it is just now. If you can't wait, look it up! I hope this book enables you to feel and do the same on your journey as I did on mine.

So, read this book with your eyes wide open and accept that your journey is not the same as everyone else's. Read this book if you're eager to learn about new concepts. Read this book with an agile mind. Please feel free to challenge the concepts, as this is something I accept. Without it, you won't make me learn. However, put into practice what is being said and you will experience enhanced success. I get told I am intelligent, but really I am not … I just love learning more than the coach and teacher down the road. That's my gift.

SECTION ONE
Warm up – Football Foundations

Section one looks into the fundamentals of what is required for elite youth performers. The eight chapters include *The Talent Myth, The 10,000 Hours of Practice Concept, Creating Winners* and *Difficult Footballers.*

CHAPTER 1

Football Irony: Bullard the Manager

"If a chairman sacks the manager he initially appointed, he should go as well." – Brian Clough

Let's be honest. Football is a drug, an epidemic in our society. It divides families, towns and cities while at the same time uniting people. Frankly, there are a lot of stupid people in and around football, and individuals without good knowledge who think they are in possession of it. Would I tell my dad how to plumb a house, which he has been doing since 1968? Instruct my mate Gary how to run his IT business, which he started in 1996? Or lecture my mum about how to educate primary school-aged children, which she did for 20 years? Of course not! But it seems that in the football industry the rule book of social etiquette goes out of the window. I mean, I don't know it all, claim to know it all or will ever know it all, but the question I'd like to pose to you is: What have I done as a job for the last 22 years? Answer: Either studying how to help people improve at sport and life, or simply making them better at sport and life. And yes, I've done that every single day for 22 years. That's what I do and that's who I am. It's what makes me get out of bed in the morning. I wasn't good enough to play elite sport, so I studied it instead.

Football is a funny industry. It's a well-known fact that the sport lacks any sort of job security.

The industry is famous for its merry-go-round of manager sackings, and they are more common than late-arriving London buses. At professional football level, it is widely acknowledged that the safest place in the system for job security is at academy level. Jobs are generally secure unless you reach a senior academy role, where unfortunately some people do lose them. I've had conversations with many senior academy managers who could develop the skill and talent to manage the first team but simply choose not to. Stress, pressure, supporters' demands and many other variables put people off the main job in the game. I have been nowhere near managing the first team of a professional football club, however, on the day I am about to describe, I was an assistant manager of the famous Isthmian Premier League Club, Leatherhead.

So, the story goes as follows … I had worked under three different managers as an assistant: Mike Sandman, Jimmy Bullard and Sammy Moore. Like any managers, all three had their strengths and weaknesses, but anyone who knows anything about non-league football will tell you that it is the budgets that generally win games over any tactical mastermind – although the managers will never admit that. I'd like to place on record how lucky I was to be part of Leatherhead's history and my relationship with the supporters will stay with me forever. At Leatherhead, I worked under Jimmy Bullard during the 2016-17 season, when he was appointed during the second month in. Wherever I am in the country, I'm often asked the same question: What was Bullard like? My answer is the same every time. I tell them:

"That man had more clarity of vision than anyone I have ever worked with. People disagreed with him about his philosophy, but he didn't care. My God, he wanted to play good football, and I regard him as a total purist in football terms."

However, there is one abiding memory from my time working with Bullard that will stay with me forever. Apart from him calling me every match day and screaming down the phone in excitement, "Sallllaaad, it's game day, my son," it is important to note that he had a very serious side. He was passionate about improving players. We had been in a relegation battle all season and the team was mostly filled with unknown kids. But, towards the end of that season, we did manage to add some class to the team. Danny Murphy, an ex Cork City full back, was as hard as nails and steadied the ship. In addition, the signing of Luke Moore, the former AFC Wimbledon player, was significant. He had the best first touch and awareness I had seen in years. Pure class. I've often said there are so many players in non-league football that cannot actually play football. Yes, you heard it; they regularly unintentionally pass the ball with their shin pad, and are more accurate with their head than they are with their feet. They run around, shout a lot and are generally just poor technical players, but during that season, Moore, Kadell Daniel, Adam Cash and Ty Smith were proper footballers who were technically as good as most professionals.

Throughout the week, Jimmy and I would often laugh nervously with each another and comment on how stressful match days were. We could never enjoy them. John Beales, our coach and Jimmy's best mate, was also in a different class. The average fan or outsider perhaps didn't realise the pride we all took in our roles. Non-league football was a part-time job after all, and results meant everything to the Leatherhead fans and us.

On the day in question, we were playing Hendon at home. This team was also in the relegation zone. As the saying goes, it was a six pointer. With just six games of the season remaining, neither side could afford to lose. We were disgraceful in the first half and were 2-0 down by the halfway stage. The half was so bad we even scored an own goal from 30 yards out, when club captain Pauly Semakula rolled the ball into his own net. At this stage, with player morale hitting the floor, I was partly convinced we were relegated. Normally, before entering the changing room for our half-time team talk, Jimmy and I had a plan of what we would say to the players. Often, the chairman, Richard Brady, would also give us feedback on what he had seen. Only on this day he swerved us, as he knew that under this sort of pressure it wasn't the time or the place for him to wade in. On this occasion, and for the first and only time we worked together, I also left Jimmy to himself. At that moment, I felt this was the right thing to do.

As an assistant, you sometimes just have to let the manager breathe. I didn't know what to expect from him, though, which had never previously been the case when we walked into the changing room. I suppose I expected him to go crazy and scream and shout like a lunatic – and like the average non-league manager who is faced with crisis and relegation. But to the contrary, Jimmy was class personified. He was upset with the players' performance, of course, but calm, purposeful, clear and focused. He went through his five or six points with the squad with complete clarity. And, before I moved onto mine, he said, "You do this, Kads, Danny, do that and float inside. Luke, get forward and create a 2v1 overload on the outside. This is how we will win this game … "

Jimmy liked how I always demanded that the players make eye contact when it was my turn to deliver my messages. (There is your first tip!) However, on this occasion, all the players had his undivided attention. In the end, we won 3-2 and Leatherhead ended the season with 24 points from 30 to stay up.

My reason for writing this chapter was to highlight the irony concerning how my time at Leatherhead ended in September 2017 – on a day I will never, ever forget. Jimmy had since left the club and joined *Soccer AM* as a presenter. I had just started my business solutionsmindset.com and I've been privileged since leaving Millwall to work with many premier league and football league players. I help, advise and support them with mental conditioning, performance and any lifestyle issues they may have. On the day I left Leatherhead, I was in Sunderland working with two premier league players on loan there. A Netflix documentary was being filmed about Sunderland's season, and the cameras were even present during my session with one of the players, whom I won't mention for now.

I have never worked for money or really been motivated by it, and this can be proved by how long I spent being a bloody teacher! I believe that if you love what you do then work isn't actually work, but we all need to pay our bills and my new business was in its infancy and flourishing, with elite athletes regularly contacting me for support. That particular day at work paid me 1000% more in one day than I earned during an entire week at Leatherhead. That day I couldn't make training and I let Sammy Moore know in the morning. Sammy was a rookie player manager, in his first job, and we had started well for the season, being fourth in the league and still on an FA cup run, which ended by getting to the second round and being televised.

CHAPTER 1 - FOOTBALL IRONY: BULLARD THE MANAGER

Whilst on the train to Sunderland, Sammy implied in a text message that he required more commitment from me, and he said he thought I should leave the club that evening. In fairness, he was under pressure as a first-time manager on a limited budget, and he felt my wages could be put to better use on the team. I was obviously upset about being forced out via text, which was mainly because I felt the decision was being pushed onto me, which it was, particularly after I had shown both him and the chairman ruthless loyalty since we had all met. I suppose I was upset that my commitment was being questioned, and anyone who knows me knows I am ruthlessly committed. However, we all have bills to pay and my burgeoning business was my priority, whereas Leatherhead, although important to me, was basically a glorified hobby. In fairness to Sammy, he was the manager and could do whatever he felt was right. Who wouldn't? In further support of his decision regarding my position, that summer I had left Millwall and missed several weeks of pre-season whilst working away with England. Again, this was not ideal, but work is work and I'd been made an offer that nobody in their right mind would refuse. I simply had to represent my country, albeit as a staff member. Sammy and I still speak and get on well, although of course I didn't agree with him letting me go in that way, as I believe flexibility around people's work issues is key in the non-league game. Most importantly, I felt I still added significant value to the team on a bigger scale.

So it was a day of complete irony. Whilst I was being employed to help two premier league football players get better at football, I was told that I could no longer help a non-league football club get better at football! Only in this sport would this happen! However, anyone who knows the football industry is fully aware of its randomness! So random in fact, I went back Leatherhead for a third time as the new director of football, meaning my love affair with the fans continued.

CHAPTER 2

Talent: The Most Overused Word in Sport

"Talent is cheaper than table salt. What separates the talented individual from the successful one is a lot of hard work."
– Stephen King

You often hear people in sport say, "Talent this, talent that." My response? "*Boring*." How many times have you heard this word used about young athletes? And sometimes about kids as young as six! One of the best player agencies I know are *Dirk Hebel Sports Consultancy* from Germany. Darren Freeman their agent always says to me, "Steve, imagine telling Ronaldo to his face that he was born and not made – he'd chin you!" They have a point.

The actual definition of talent is as follows: - "(Someone who has) a natural ability to be good at something, especially without being taught."

The above definition may well sound exciting to the average parent, but to me it's mind numbing. Put simply, talent without the application and commitment to work hard is pointless. If you went through the statistics concerning the promising schoolboy players who have gone on to achieve a professional status over the last 30 years, you would be alarmed. And not just in the world of football ... I mean any sport. Therefore, being the best at 15 years old could be seen as a waste of time. What we know about teenagers is that they are more likely than adults to become wayward in their behaviour. In terms of gender, boys are physiologically designed to achieve less than girls. Scientific research on the brain has shown that boys are risk takers. The reason I'm saying this is because if you use football as an example, when talented young men achieve a bit of success, they often don't have the emotional intelligence to harness their talent. After all, they've not really been required to work hard thus far on their journey to achieve what, if we're honest, equates to just a small amount of success. I truly believe that most young people do not mentally correlate their futures with any sort of hard work. Consequently, this is a dangerous position for them to be in and family support is vital.

I have found that numpties surround many of these boys.

These include:

- Clueless parents who live their life through their child, and see them as a potential pay packet and pension scheme.
- Agents who possess no life skills whatsoever yet offer advice to kids they are unqualified to give.
- Friends who distract them with poor behaviour, which negatively affects training and focus.
- Coaches who misguide them with inaccurate knowledge, guidance and advice that is the result of either a lack of understanding or, worse, a need to make themselves look good at the expense of the welfare and future of the athlete.

So, *what are the solutions* to harness the talent of these kids?

- Firstly, do not blow smoke in or around them! Remember, these young people see themselves as having proven themselves just by doing things as normal. Often, unless they're mentored properly, they won't understand about failure and its correlation to resilience – often, they will not have failed at anything as yet. As an example, scoring three goals every week while playing with their own age group could be seen as pointless, but it does have an important role in allowing them to spend time with their peer group and maintain good friendships.
- Secondly, from a technical and developmental point of view, it could be seen as flawed. At this stage in their development, they simply need to focus on getting better and improving, because improving means experiencing failure and failure can mean playing against

a far superior opposition. After all, they have proved themselves plenty by now with their own age group, so to move onto the next stage they need to be stretched and challenged.

So, what do we mean by improving?

One big example involves putting the athlete in a situation where training and match days will make them fail. Yes, you heard it. Stop making your sessions so clean. You need to ensure they find out what failure looks and feels like, and encourage reflection concerning their next steps. This is about helping athletes retrain their mind in order to grasp that success is not a given for them. I've heard and read nonsense many times about learning and how it has to be nice, fluffy and clean-looking. Life is not clean and fluffy so why should we pretend to young people that sport is?

> *Simply put, the harder we make it for them, the more chance the 'talented' players will have of achieving success in the long term.*

Let's be honest here, too much too soon has never worked. Now, in contrast, please keep in mind that this theory isn't going to work for the less talented athletes. In order to improve, they need extra support. There is no point in continually letting them drown. These less able athletes are often very committed but just haven't got the 'X factor' that is needed for district, county or academy level. Therefore, you need to be softer. In summary, think about these four aspects concerning the athletes you serve.

Are they:

- High in talent and high in commitment?
- High in talent and low in commitment?
- Low in talent and high in commitment?
- Low in talent and low in commitment?

Remember, you really need to think about context. If the child has little talent then it's unlikely they will ever play sport professionally. However, you don't want to put them off their love for the sport, as they may well play recreationally in the future. Pushing these types of kids too hard is often destined for failure. In contrast, if the 'talented' athlete cannot cope with the high demands you place on them by deliberately making life hard, and they end up quitting, then at least this has happened early on, because if they cannot cope now they are unlikely to at a higher level. Believe it or not, it isn't every young athlete's dream to play professionally, even though you may think they want it just like you used to. Uniquely, many young people I have spoken to don't see elite sport as their only way in life. Therefore, it's vital to have a frank discussion with talented athletes early in their adolescent career and explain clearly to them how hard the upcoming journey is going to be.

If the talented athlete has a high commitment level then the only barrier to them succeeding would be pure bad luck. This often includes their genetics or injuries that may hinder that journey.

CHAPTER 3

Winners! How do you Create Them?

REDGEs: Players that are 'Rounded' BUT with an 'Edge'

"Losers make promises they often break. Winners make commitments they always keep." – Denis Waitley

I stole the term 'REDGE' from Dr Mark Nesti of *Liverpool John Moores University*. In 2015, while attending an elite player development conference, the topic of discussion was: What football academies crave from the character of players, and what they need in order to be successful at the top level.

After all, amongst a room full of Academy Managers and Heads of Education, we all knew what we did and didn't want:

- ✗ Difficult people in the building.
- ✓ Rounded and holistically minded athletes.

The second bullet point is one that we all felt helped athletes become successful. And then, Nesti discussed a story of the Everton Academy kit man who, during a meeting, yelled something out from his kit room. As the story goes, the meeting was in full flow and the Everton staff members were discussing the importance of having rounded players as part of character development. At this moment, the kit man suddenly shouted out from down the corridor, "Yes, but they need an edge." Although the Everton FC staff wanted a modern-day and 'new school' type of athlete, who behaved well in and around the building (which was holistically the model of the complete player), they still agreed that day that having an edge is a massive part of an elite athlete's repertoire. I don't know of anyone who would argue with this method for creating the best and most elite athletes – and that is why I love the term.

Following the Euro 2016 football tournament, England players were heavily criticised for their failure to perform and succeed, which ended with a defeat to Iceland, a country that had a population of only 334,000 people compared to our 55 million (at the time). No one involved in elite coaching and development has the one given answer regarding why England did not fulfil their potential at the tournament, or many others in recent decades for that matter. But this is my point, and like most teams or individuals who do not succeed in sport, there is always a multitude of variables, of small or big reasons. The saying 'one percenters' is relevant in failure, and I am obsessed with using it because it compartmentalises performance for athletes and breaks it down into chunks, which they will see can eventually add up over time.

It frustrates me greatly when I hear:"*We are not technical in English football.*" I believe that over the years we have had many technically efficient players. I also believe that another reason for our country's potential being stifled at international level is that some media pundits and journalists refuse to help the cause. Basically, they are businessmen and women trying to sell newspapers. Following the disastrous Iceland defeat, the trend in the media was that England players now needed, "Psychological support to make us better."

I don't disagree with this statement and I am hoping to start my doctorate in sport psychology soon. However, for me, football players across all levels of the game need one major ingredient that isn't necessarily psychological intervention, but rather intellectual support and intervention. Examples regarding my hypothesis include: *problem-solving* and *decision-making skills, intra-personal* and *inter-personal skills* and *coping with emotional pressure in the game*, to name but a few.

> *Educators often look at individual player development, but surely group dynamic training is what's missing.*

If they want to be successful, these players need to understand their teammates, not to mention themselves, better. It was clear that the 2018 World Cup squad was far more unified and that a genuinely impactful strategy had been put into place.

Now, most people 'in the know' are aware that teaching and learning interventions could easily be described as sport psychology interventions, as the crossovers are vast. So, let me start with a fictional example of what can happen to our young elite players involved in football clubs across the UK:

A player at 14 is signed for £500,000. They're given:

- ✓ Training kit, free boots, trainers and school fees
- ✓ The best pitches
- ✓ Coaching and facilities
- ✓ A new home
- ✓ A kit man to wash their kit every day
- ✓ Physiological, technical and tactical support
- ✓ Psychological support, but all performance-related, right?

Without stating the obvious, shouldn't it be life-related? As a former Head of Education and Player Welfare of a championship football club, that was technically my job. I know only too well the demands of the role. Sadly, however, the bureaucracy of the EPPP (Elite Player Performance Plan) during my last two years in the role meant that I spent all my days on a laptop having to prove what I was doing, instead of improving the lives of the players I was supposed to be serving with face-to-face interaction. As a positive, I have always said the EPPP got rid of the blaggers but sadly stifled the innovators. Moving forwards, I believe this is something that needs to be looked at, otherwise the elite game is going to lose some really good people.

How much genuine and rigorous mentoring happens with these top players?

I've said it before and I will say it again: the majority of those involved in the football industry know a lot about 11v11 on the football pitch, but not much about anything else. People at the top at various big clubs around the world still don't understand this part of the youth development journey. At the training ground of an underachieving club, all you often hear is football this, football that … everything is about football. My advice? Be careful what you deliver.

Remember that *no matter where in the world they live*, people are pretty similar. The facts are, we are born, we live and then we all die. We all experience fear, worry and anxiety and, at the other end of the scale, we know what it's like to feel happiness, contentment and love. In life, it is common for famous people, such as pop stars, sportsmen and women and fashion models to be defined by something they are good at. Sadly, however, this success masks the real person behind the star. Witnessing them are young, elite players who often haven't achieved much in their careers so far and thus get sucked into an identity crisis. They need reminding on a daily basis how little they have accomplished so far, yet we persist in thinking that giving them the best of everything so young is really going to help them. Is it heck! I know that sounds harsh, but it is entirely, factually and objectively true. My advice, therefore, is that these young people need the right people around them to give them the correct advice from early on.

It's as if these young people can gain celebrity status without actually achieving anything. We only have to look at the amount of fallen stars there have been over the last couple of decades to know that this development methodology isn't accurate or appropriate for the vast majority. The reason horror stories happen in football is because many of the people in charge of the clubs and the academies may know a lot about the beautiful game but *very little* about child development. In actual fact, it is miles away from where it needs to be. It is like putting a university professor in charge of an infant school. The skillset required, although seemingly similar, does not correlate in reality. Playing 500 league games does not qualify someone to be in charge of a child's development, unless, may I add, they portray the behaviours to do so. Knowing about football isn't enough, which is why so much bad practice goes on, and the best clubs nail it perfectly. What I will say is that youth development is now at its peak in England and there are many skilled people in the right places. What I really worry about is the effects of practices like 'day release' and moving kids across the country to attend new schools, etc. I think these need to be examined more closely before we let them continue.

So, what is my advice to teenage athletes with potential who have been purchased for large amounts of money? Well, it's that you need early intervention. This includes mentoring, life coaching, performance and lifestyle advice and educational support. This should be provided by the right people from day one (not cowboys or unskilled agents who claim they have walked the walk – they need to have done the walking). Similar to making progress in life, learning to become an elite athlete is hard to adjust to, and it's not formed with 'magic spray dust' or by fluke!

Let's get this straight, given that we know the obvious: Teenagers turn into adults.

I'm happy to be called mad, but my view is that giving young people the best too early (and not just when it comes to sport) isn't the best way to produce sustained and elite performance outcomes for modern-day athletes. Those who work with young people and those who have children of their own are well aware that, even at the best of times, young people will cut corners and get LAZY. So, if we know this about children, why are many sports organisations giving these kids too much too young? I see it as immoral and unethical. I appreciate that in football the competition for players' signatures is tough for clubs and they have to protect themselves, but there must be another way to go about it. Why are people in the industry allowed to get away with a flawed strategy towards these kids and their families year after year? In 2015, I heard one academy manager from a premier league club liken the strategies some clubs used for their young athletes to child abuse.

So, how can we make life harder for athletes, without hindering them? I'm not advocating being horrible to children, but we know that the saying, 'Short term pain for long term gain' actually works. It is the way it should be. The saying, 'tough love' is also prominent in this context. Again, I'm not talking about child neglect or cruelty; I'm referring to a structure, strategy and thought-out philosophy surrounding:

- ✓ The definition of development for young athletes.
- ✓ What it LOOKS and FEELS like for them.

This is *not* about:

- ✗ Giving them big contracts too early
- ✗ Boot deals
- ✗ Great facilities
- ✗ Giving them the wrong messages regarding what it takes to be an elite player in the future

For years, clubs have been giving hundreds of thousands of pounds to these young people. Now, get ready for my tag line:

> So many of these kids don't make it as a professional player at any level anyway!

Wow, I say. I mean, really? I appreciate that the heads of academies do not hold the purse strings, but surely some of the people in these clubs' hierarchies must be more accountable.

Surely a *better strategy* is to say to a family/player:

"Firstly, if you do not like what we offer you, you can simply leave and go and play elsewhere. But what we will do for you is the following:

- ✓ Care about you the most
- ✓ Coach you the best

- ✓ Give you a full performance and non-performance programme, which is truly holistic and involves career pathways outside of football."

The club should then say:

"And if you choose to 'get on the bus' and come on this journey with us, and if you then get into the first team and play 50 games, we will (as an example) provide some pro-rata back pay at double the usual amount!"

That would incentivise anyone to keep working hard, wouldn't it? Now, before you jump on me, and pronounce my examples as ludicrous and unattainable, I just want you to see it as my way of highlighting the importance of earning what you have worked for.

Just looking at a short-term financial fix is a dangerous process for any young person. How can we create that rounded player with an edge if all we keep doing is making those edges softer to touch and easier to ignore. Too much, too soon has to stop. It ain't working! However, what I will say is well done to all those clubs that refuse to follow convention and put a cap on their young players' wage structure. If I was involved at management level at an academy again, the kit man would be long gone and the youth team would be doing this work themselves! Why? Because you have to make young people do things they do not want to do. It is life. Welcome to the real world, I say!

In summary, making teenagers do a lot of things they normally wouldn't trouble themselves with is helpful to them in the long term, because then when the tough stuff hits them, they will have already learnt to cope emotionally, intellectually and, most importantly, with *positivity*. After all, being successful has *never* been easy, so why are some of the people in charge of youth development making it so?

CHAPTER 4

How to Achieve Success: A Young Athlete's Approach

"If you set your goals ridiculously high and it's a failure, you will fail above everyone else's success." – James Cameron

Over my lifetime, I've had many conversations with young people. That's no surprise really, although in the last few years, my journey has taken a slightly different path and my days now entail supporting elite athletes and business people. I recently counted that I have taught approximately 30,000 children. The conversations we've had have been in both formal and informal settings and they've been about what it takes to be successful in academia, relationships and, believe it or not, even love. I noted recently that I have formally taught young people from the age of four all the way up to university. When I reflected about my experiences as a professional, I realised that throughout my career I have taught the following subjects: football, rugby, tennis, table tennis, trampolining, handball, basketball, korfball, gymnastics, GCSE Dance, GCSE PE, A Level PE, BTEC PE, half course GCSE PE, degree level PE, Sports Leadership Awards, orienteering, cycling, cricket, athletics, netball, health-related fitness, volleyball, softball, badminton, rounders, squash, canoeing, golf, hockey, rowing, swimming, maths, geography and science. That's a total of 36 separate disciplines that have made me the man I am today. Was I great at teaching them all? Of course not, but my point is that these experiences are not the norm, and they have moulded me into the practitioner I am today. I can safely say that the average football coach hasn't had these experiences and won't fully understand what learning is and what it looks like for athletes.

I recently delivered a sport psychology module to a group of under-18 players at a professional club. These were some of their responses to my starter question, which was: How can we achieve our goals and become successful?

The top answers were:

- Be on time
- Be an individual and express yourself
- Be a good learner
- Be prepared to accept others' views and compare them to your own
- Failing to prepare is preparing to fail
- Work hard during every session
- Have desire and a vision
- Set targets
- Use your spare time wisely
- Be positive and resilient

To be honest, from experience, these sayings mean very little to me. Why? Well, they are merely words on a page. And it's rare for young people to genuinely interpret the meaning of them and then implement them in their daily behaviour. I always say to athletes, "Actions not blag." I'm sure most people reading this book who are either parents or work with young people can relate to this.

For example:

- ✓ **Hard work** – The young people who make these statements are often unaware of the following: How does hard work feel? What does it look like? This is because most kids don't like hard work.
- ✓ **Using time wisely** – What does that look and feel like for a young person? Most kids are late!
- ✓ **Being positive and resilient** – Again, these are just words. What

does resilient feel and look like for a young person? I.e. can resilience be learnt and improved? Most kids give up easily.

- ✓ **Setting targets** – How do you set targets? Why do you set targets? How do you measure these to help you improve? Most kids are used to saying, "whatevs" and they don't care like their parents do!

- ✓ **Desire and a vision for success** – Can you teach this to young people? If you can't then you can certainly discuss it and create a dialogue with them. That's a start. Are the best athletes born or made with desire? Most kids normally desire a quick fix to success.

So, to summarise, when you say to a young person all of the above, I generally believe it is nowhere near rigorous enough. You have to purposefully build in a *'scaffolded process'* so these young athletes can **ACCESS** what you are saying to them as easy as it is to eat candyfloss. Scaffolded learning basically means breaking down teaching into chunks so that students can really comprehend what you are saying. Otherwise the words you say will be meaningless, pointless and cloudy.

If you at least attempt all of the above, then these young people will be more likely to achieve success.

CHAPTER 5

The Mario Balotelli Effect and 'Difficult' Footballers

Blame him? Or the people that helped create him?

"Many stories are invented about me – too many stories; almost everyone uses me, and I'd say about 0.01 per cent of the gossip is true." – Mario Balotelli

As a behaviour specialist for many years, I learnt very early in my career the following statement:

"Every behaviour needs a consequence, good and bad."

And Balotelli, along with many other 'difficult' footballers, has made a great impact on the world game – sadly often in the *wrong way*. Balotelli intrigues me and I would love to have been part of his journey, as I truly believe I could have helped him.

So, why does football seem to have *more* of these types of people compared to other sports?

Balotelli has almost become more famous for his off-the-field antics than he has for his performances on the pitch. There is no denying that he's highly controversial and he's talked about in changing rooms, pubs and offices across the world.

On many occasions, he's stated that he has been treated unfairly by his managers and the media, but his behaviour seems to be a problem wherever he goes. In the past, his good performances have justified him being allowed to play at a top level, and, despite all the negative press around him at these times, he has still started matches for his team week in week out. What are your thoughts on this? Should he still have started matches? Forgetting Balotelli here …

- Are the £100,000 per week-plus salaries of the players justified when some of them display consistently poor behaviour?
- Is this the type of behaviour we want from a role model in our society?
- Do managers, chairmen and women and board members even care about the disruptive influence of players?
- Are results all that matter at the top level?

Balotelli's record for being signed by many clubs and then released or sold shortly afterwards suggests that managers simply see the player first and not the man behind the player. These managers want to keep their jobs and are in desperate need to win games at any cost. Some of Balotelli's previous managers have put his volatile behaviour down to his young age. But is someone's age always a valid excuse for the mistakes they make in life? I'll let you decide …

> Difficult players do not just exist at the top level of the game. Forget football here, remember that difficult PEOPLE exist everywhere.

But why are people in all walks of life difficult and challenging?

Have you ever spent any time truly analysing difficult people and why they portray the traits they do? A study conducted at the University of Edinburgh found that a young person who had been permanently excluded from secondary school by the age of 12 was four times more likely to go to prison. Therefore, early intervention for these young people is a priority and, referring back to sport, the list of difficult athletes is endless so we need to help them earlier with a clear rewards and sanctions process. Remember that sport in general is a powerful tool for human change. Boxing and martial arts are well known to enhance discipline and that's something footballers can benefit from. In fact, if the football industry opened its eyes sooner to what's going on elsewhere, I truly believe the game in this country would be in a better place. A decade ago, Clive Woodward, the England Rugby guru, almost got laughed out of Southampton Football Club for turning his attention to the beautiful game, but he now speaks at premier league conferences and educates footy people on how to create elite environments. Oh, the irony.

In youth sport in particular, the blame culture of poor behaviour can often be targeted at the athlete instead of the people (or the so-called experts) in charge of their development: the coach, teacher or parent. People often assume that our society is naturally equal. We are all born the same way, of course, but then as we grow up our environments and narratives move apart. I call this your map. We all have different maps, so if Balotelli had a map from childhood that told him he would persistently get away with poor behaviour, well, that would explain how he conducts himself today.

In an ideal world, we are all supposed to behave like the following:

- ✓ With good social values
- ✓ Correctly and with good manners
- ✓ With moral soundness.

However, is this achievable without the correct guidance, support, care and intervention?

In my university lecturing days, I once mentored a student teacher who simply wasn't destined for his chosen career. I felt guilty saying this about someone so early on in their career, but sadly that was the truth. Much to my bewilderment, I wasn't even sure he liked the company of children, which certainly didn't help his cause. I reached my conclusion after observing him during a Year 8 basketball lesson. No learning could take place as the kids answered back, fought with each other and generally displayed an appalling group attitude. This destroyed the flow of the lesson but also the teacher's mindset and confidence in the process. His inexperience was really beginning to show and an hour or so later it was time to give him some feedback in the PE office. We had a very frank discussion, but unfortunately it didn't pan out the way I thought it would. Put it this way, he had a shock for me. We were now on week 10 of his teacher-training placement and normally at this stage, I expect to see consistent rules and regulations concerning school policy and good practice being implemented. Up to that point, I had mentored about 100 trainees so I was crystal clear regarding where my current one should be in terms of quality and skills.

Basic things were not being implemented, such as:

- Pupils lining up in a straight line and in silence before the lesson.
- Getting changed in four minutes, as per the school policy.
- The class completing an independent warm up without teacher support.
- Employing the 'behaviour for learning' strategies we had previously set as professional targets.
- All pupils following instructions first time round.
- And if the above were not adhered to, an immediate sanction being put in place (three warnings process, detention, parent phone call, etc.)

OK, OK, so he had tried to implement a few of the above but had failed miserably for the tenth week running. In fact, from the start of the lesson the pupils ran riot. The situation was becoming unsafe and when I asked him how he thought the lesson had gone, unbelievably he was none the wiser and he looked at me like I was mad. He basically blamed the pupils for everything. Yes, you heard it:

> *An adult, who had chosen inner-city teaching as a career, was on week 10 of his placement and was blaming everything and everyone other than himself for the poor behaviour of the class. Self-awareness alert right there!*

So, to reiterate my point about Balotelli, people can blame him and similar players all they want, but my experience tells me otherwise. In the schools I worked in, poor behaviour was commonplace and we didn't just wipe our hands of them and let them get away with poor conduct. As the qualified adults, we educated, nurtured, rewarded, sanctioned, mentored and coached them in the process of how to behave.

The main job in inner city schools these days is to educate young people on how to behave better in order to impact learning, using the various strategies available. In the short term, a sanction or quick punishment is normally key in order to set boundaries. This often fails in the medium and long term, as young people can only be punished for so long before they rebel and show regular defiance towards the draconian regime. In more middle class areas across the country, it probably doesn't matter how autocratic things are because the kids just do as they are told anyway. The inner city is so different. This is mainly due to the kids carrying an initial lack of trust and respect for their teachers and the institution they work for.

So my questions to you are:

- Why do Balotelli and other athletes historically act in this way?
- Who were Balotelli's mentors and guides as a youngster?
- What was his childhood background?
- Was he let off time and time again for poor conduct just because he was good at football?
- Did staff accept his poor behaviour in search of the short-term fix of the three points and victory on match day?
- What sanctions did he receive as a child and into adulthood that made him understand a consequence would be implemented for his poor actions?
- Was a mentoring/life-coaching programme put in place for him? And if not, why not?

At the very start of this book, I stated how I would provide you with as many questions as I would answers. In summary, there are lots of thoughts for you to reflect on. But my main point is that before you start blaming the kids that turn into difficult adults, start blaming the adults that are in charge of them!

CHAPTER 6

The 10,000 Hours of Practice Rule!

(And my reasons why it will never work in football!)

"In fact, researchers have settled on what they believe is the magic number for true expertise: ten thousand hours." – Malcolm Gladwell

Is it true, or mythical nonsense? Some of you reading this may have heard the above numerical term before and read the research about what it takes, in terms of practice hours, to be an elite athlete. In recent years, the former British table tennis star, Olympian and now author, Matthew Syed, discussed his sporting journey in his book *Bounce*. He also debated the many theories about how to become an elite athlete.

Syed's research took him far and wide and it originated from years earlier when the journalist, author and speaker Malcom Gladwell conducted research on the 10,000 hours theory for his book *Outliers*. Gladwell has mentioned several times that the key to success in any field is the notion of 10,000 hours of deliberate practice, which, potentially, 'makes the perfect athlete'. He makes examples of The Beatles and Bill Gates and how they achieved 'early learning access' to their eventual field of expertise in music and IT programming, respectively. He claims the hours they committed eventually led to them being successful. What do you think about this? Does practice make perfect, or is success destined from birth?

I don't think that anyone could argue against the fact that practising your trade helps you perform better and improve.

But, does practising for this amount of time:

A. Guarantee a professional contract at the end point of the practice journey?

Or

B. Create a world-class performer?

I personally find this hard to agree with, acknowledge and understand. I often ask myself why I feel this way, and maybe it is because of all of the bad practice in teaching, coaching and performance support that I have witnessed in my career.

An example of the bad teaching I have witnessed is substandard science teachers asking pupils to conduct experiments over a two to three year exam period. Depressingly, some of these teachers could have been with these students for ten years and incorporated 50,000 hours of teaching and they still wouldn't have learnt anything significant. This is down to the uselessness of the teachers in question. Sorry to bash science teachers, but recruiting good ones is notoriously hard.

In contrast, I've seen some expert teachers double the skills and intelligence of their pupils in half the allotted time compared with an average teacher. This is simply down to one thing: great teaching! For years, I witnessed football coaches educating inadequately and often causing the players they were 'helping' to get worse!

There used to be a national coaching strategy with a tag line that went, *'Let the game be the teacher.'* I mean, seriously, what a load of cobblers that was! Yes, that's right (note my sarcasm), let the expert with all this knowledge:

- Say nothing
- Impart no information
- Let kids learn through a game scenario in the wrong way for 10,000 hours. I basically call this creativity gone wrong.

I laugh at this type of educational methodology, as the learner often then has to spend their entire lifetime unlearning bad techniques and decision making because they weren't taught properly in the first place. There is maverick coaching and there is stupidity. Precious time is often wasted on true, authentic and effective learning. Trust me on this, good teachers and coaches are gold dust and they need to be identified immediately by their bosses and kept at their respective clubs and schools at all costs.

It makes me laugh when old pros speak on the radio about how they developed as children back in the '60s and '70s by "free play in the street". When will they understand that the game has moved on and that technical coaching from an early age is paramount in the modern game. There will always be success anomalies in sport, but generally a good schooling in any sporting industry is vital.

So, in summary, the quality of the practice is key to success, and it's not necessarily about doing hours and hours of practice at something, which, as I've emphasised, you may be practising badly.

Now, what is my point about the title of this topic?

Earlier, I confidently stated that the 10,000-hours rule in the world of practice, whether it be in sports, music or otherwise, categorically will not make you a guaranteed expert. Surely some people are simply born with these various skills? Views differ around the world, of course, and I am not sure how you interpret this topic and how it relates to a sport like football. I believe that the variables in invasion game sports like football, hockey, netball and rugby are so vast that it's sometimes almost impossible to predict a pathway for an athlete.

So, what do I mean by practice variables?

In particular, by comparing sport to music as an example and, in greater detail, comparing the more closed skill sports, such as snooker, table tennis and darts, with other sports that have a greater process to change in terms of the performance environment. I first learnt about this topic while studying for an A Level in Physical Education, and it always inspires great debate around the skill acquisition theory, as studied by the Dreyfus brothers in 1980.

Initially, let me explain the unique difference between open and closed skills and sports.

> **Open Skills and Sports**

Basically, changes in the environment happen a LOT in these skills/sports. This makes the chances of becoming a professional much slimmer. Examples include:

- ✓ *Windsurfing:* Each second, the changing wind and wave direction means that new decisions have to be made. Most importantly, different skills and decisions need to be made over and over again. Therefore, almost every single second of action equals more variables.

- ✓ *A football match:* It's usually 11 versus 11, but there is often a different-sized pitch, different formations for your team, different teammates every game; 11 different opponents every week that play in different formations and in different positions. In addition, play may be on different surfaces, with different weather and climate changes equalling more variables.

- ✓ *Orienteering:* This encompasses weather changes and the course is different for every competition, as is the map they read.

> **Closed Skills and Sports**

The skills and games that involve fewer variables make them easier to master. Examples include:

- ✓ *Playing the piano:* The piano never changes size or moves as you play it. You play it alone and the notes you play sound the same every time.

- ✓ *Snooker:* The table size never changes or moves, nor do the pockets. The ball(s) you are aiming for stays in position, as does the ball you hit it with.

- ✓ *Table Tennis:* This requires lower aerobic effort compared to elite invasion games. The table size never changes, the net never moves, the game is always played indoors and weather is never an issue.

So, to finish off this chapter, I urge you to think about and reflect on the variables of football and invasion games in general, in comparison to other sports. We know that the process of skill acquisition in practice is important, but I believe that the 10,000-hour rule in relation to invasion games will never be an accurate assessment and method for expertise because far more decisions need to be made in these sports than, say, table tennis, darts or snooker. Success in football not only requires physical and genetic advantages, but also the ability to deal with so many more variables. Statistically, players only have the ball for two to three minutes of a 90-minute game; therefore, what are they doing for the other 88 minutes?

- Thinking a lot
- Running a lot
- Communicating a lot
- Making decisions a lot

Manchester United Academy Manager, Nick Cox, once said to a large audience of football professionals, including me:

> *"Player development should be about 10,000 experiences over their academy lifetime, and not 10,000 hours."*

CHAPTER 7

What is Development in Football for Youth Athletes?

"Create an environment where champions are inevitable."
– Vern Gambetta

We've all said things to our friends like this:

- "This coach is great, but that other one is rubbish."
- "That coach is crap, because he just shouts at us all the time."
- "You should coach players this way, the way I have shown you, not that way, you're wrong."
- "This club is the best place for youth development … but that club is rubbish, don't play for them."
- "Don't sign for them, their manager is an idiot and the club's ethos is poor."

So, *what needs to be done in order for athletes to be a success?*

Do you:

- Send your son or daughter to a top premier league club with the best facilities and financial backing?
- Send them to a lower league club knowing that the path to the first team is much more realistic and potentially easier to achieve, and they get to play every week?

I suppose it entirely depends on what you think development is and what it looks like.

So:

- Do great facilities create elite performers, or do the people and staff have the most influence on excellence?
- Does a strategy and process help produce and develop a footballer, or is success in the game down to luck?

I believe it all comes down to the athlete and their family's personal preference. Players and their support networks would be wrong to think that there are better quality coaches at the top clubs compared to the lower leagues. It's a bit like a high-end school I suppose. Great teachers and coaches exist everywhere, not just in the best-looking buildings. In the early 2000s, Martin Hinshelwood, Dean Wilkins and Vic Bragg created an academy legacy at Brighton and Hove Albion. The facilities the club had at the time were shocking, and everyone lived out of Portakabins, but they still managed to produce several seasoned professionals that had solid careers, including Dean Hammond, Dean Cox, Dan Harding, Tommy Elphick, Adam Hinshelwood, Adam El-Abd, Adam Virgo, Joel Lynch, Tommy Fraser, Jake Robinson and Lewis Dunk, who all represented the club at first-team level. This was a truly unbelievable achievement by the club, which had crap resources and facilities but achieved success thanks to the incredible staff and culture.

Have you ever wondered whether the better schools around the world have the best teachers? I'll let you decide, but here's a little hint ... NO CHANCE! I have got loads of personal evidence to back up my opinion.

If families think excellent facilities are the be all and end all to help their child improve then they are wrong. If families think facilities can help an athlete have a greater chance of glory then they could be right.

But remember the title of this chapter. It depends on what you see development *as* in the first place.

Here are some further questions for you to ponder:

- Do the substandard facilities and infrastructure in Brazil prevent the nation's footballers from being technically great?

> Do the great facilities at St George's Park, the home of English football, mean we will produce better players?

My own answer to the latter is who knows, but it seems to be working. May I add that the coaches at club level across the country need a pat on the back for producing the players that hit the level required for international standard. Well done to all the staff who contribute to making our country great; it is always a team effort.

Keep in mind that risk versus reward is not in an aspiring footballer's favour. Just think about all the money spent on travel, the family time that gets decimated, the friendships that become tarnished and the school grades that drop due to the extraordinary commitment required of academy players. And all for the small chance of becoming a professional footballer. My rough estimations are as follows. There are 92 professional clubs in England and there has only ever been this number of league clubs. This means that we have about 3,500 to 4000 professional players in this country. The latest statistics show that about six million boys and men play football. By my reckoning, the chances of becoming a professional football player for a living, from birth, are approximately 0.06%. This may be a minor statistic, but it's hugely important to know, and I'd hazard a guess that many parents up and down the country won't have a clue about these numbers. I am not trying to lower the aspiration of elite youth footballers out there, but the facts are there for all to see. Being a professional footballer for 10 years or more is unlikely, so my advice is to make sure the journey along the way is fun!

Competition or friendly matches?

I believe that one area of the game that needs a revamp and needs to meet a 'middle ground' at academy and grassroots-level is competition strategy. As an example, academy players from nine to 16 years old basically play friendlies for seven years. Honestly, what is that all about? Complete nonsense if you ask me. Now, I'm not saying that winning is everything, because it most certainly isn't, but if I made the decisions it would be half a season of friendlies and the other half spent in league competition. I would also introduce the same strategy to the grassroots game, where I believe too much emphasis is placed on winning, which is mainly because parents think their lost childhood can be redeemed through that of their offspring, and therefore proper player development is hindered because of an all-round obsession with results and trophies. In short, most of us know that learning to win is development within itself and should be embraced, as should learning to lose, may I add. I call this methodology the *prove or improve process*.

What is more important at youth level: to win games, or just get better and improve? Who knows, as both are important, but I believe an 80/20 process has to be viewed; 80% on development and a 20% focus on how development can get you success.

So, I'll summarise this chapter by sharing an experience. When staff, players or parents approach me for advice on a player development pathway, I pretty much always give the same answer, which is:

"As long as you have a plan and a strategy, I don't care what you do."

- Development is *not* concrete or fixed.
- There is *no single way* to achieve stardom.
- Sometimes, two people with different opinions on what is needed for success can *both be right*.

I can't stand it when I hear horror stories of how athletes have been coached, managed and developed with:

- Made up rules.
- Poor thoughts from coaches about the long-term effects of impulsive, short-term decisions.
- The coach allowing his own emotions to overpower the needs of the athletes.
- A narrow-minded approach to holistic development in general.

I do not claim to have all the answers, but my advice to you all would be to start:

"Thinking about thinking ... being a better developer."

CHAPTER 8

3 Point Football: Performance Where it Counts

"Winning is habit. Unfortunately, so is losing." – Vince Lombardi

We've all discussed this topic before.

What's the best pathway for athletes involved in elite sport who are trying to make it to the top of their profession?

- Do they sit in the reserves, development squads or, at professional football level, the under 23s and hope to move up the pecking order?

Or

- Is it more beneficial to take a drop in standard and get the opportunity and real-life experiences to play first-team football lower down the pyramid?

The second way means gaining the experience of 'playing for three points' every week, and choosing this pathway means playing in games that truly mean something, increasing the pressure on players to prove themselves week after week and under greater fan scrutiny.

I suppose the main question is: *What do you perceive to be the best development pathway?* Having had these conversations for years, I can honestly say that an athlete's career can often end up in the hands of the wrong people. In terms of player loans, the many examples of what is talked about and discussed with regards to player development at professional football level can go a little like this:

- It might mean that you want a flashy and arrogant player who needs to be taken down a peg or two in terms of mindset and attitude.

If they drop a few leagues they will experience fewer resources in terms of poorer pitches and training facilities. This will, as I call it, build up their mentality to reality.

- Alternatively, you might want to send a player to a deliberately 'old school' manager who puts verbal and aggressive demands on the players. The footballers in question will usually respond in the opposite way to how they've been told, which will test them and build up their resilience.
- Thirdly, you may want a highly technical player to go to a technically minded manager lower down the leagues so they can revisit the learning you have provided at your club, but at an easier standard to perform at.
- Finally, you might want a psychologically weaker player to develop their resilience under a 'new school' manager who likes to nurture their players and uses modern tactics as their main helping strategy.

Whichever strategy you pick, simply having one is a priority for an athlete's destiny.

Often in the football industry, players get loaned out to play for a lower league team, with the decision made with no strategy behind it at all. It is often a favour to a fellow manager, or because the player just needs match minutes to keep up their fitness levels. I get all of these types of decisions of course, and I understand that it's more common at the lower end of the game where needs must at times for quick wins. However, here I am referring to the top end of elite-level sport, where every under 18 and under 23 player should have, at the very least, a planned journey laid out for them by the head coach. This includes a timeline strategy, with a plan created for them by their managers and coaches regarding what their development pathway is going to look like. And, most importantly, once this has been done, there should be discussions between the player and coach as to why it is going to look like that.

The Learning Journey Mapped Out

Obviously, plans and strategies for elite performers in any workplace require a flexible approach. That's obvious, but the term learning journey exists for a reason. It's a journey. When people travel abroad they usually know their itinerary, right? They know where their journey will start and where it will end. Sometimes on that journey things happen that they did not expect, such as delayed flights or hotel rooms being double booked. These external influences force you to adapt. My argument is that at the elite level of any sport, each and every player in any professional environment should have a clear idea about what is expected of them in the next two, three or four years of their contract. And, in order to get a 'joint buy in', the player needs to understand how the staff will help them achieve their outcomes.

So often in the football industry, made up rules occur from week to week. These can be flawed or simply lack substance. Often, decisions about players are made based on emotion instead of a well thought-out process. Players in all sports appreciate it when their leaders have a vision for them and monitor the progress they make together. It makes athletes feel valued and cared for. I was privileged to be part of the England under 15 selection camp and player reviews, which was a process that lasted two full days. What was so refreshing was that the staff around the table portrayed detailed, calm, solid and consistent thoughts throughout all our in-depth conversations.

We all know players who have excelled by taking one step back and then two steps forward. There was Jamie Vardy recently and Ian Wright back in the '90s, and don't forget Paul Pogba, who was let go by Manchester United only to be resigned years later for 105 million euros. Kevin De Bruyne was released by Chelsea to get first-team opportunities elsewhere. Years later, he ended up at Manchester City, as the more refined star he is today. This method does work for many players. In contrast, the biggest ethical worry comes from the huge numbers of academy players who have salaries that don't correlate with any actual success. They play and train daily in development games with the best facilities and pitches. They play a utopian style of football that looks like it's come out of a textbook. Their fellow competitors are normally of the same age and experience (football and life), but basically at a different club down the road. The games they play are competitive and the players do, of course, get to develop in a variety of different ways. But remember, these games are mostly held in pristine and glossy training grounds. There are no paying fans heckling their every bad pass or cheering their every tackle, and the setup does not include a manager who will lose his job if the three points aren't delivered. In my opinion, these challenging external factors simply cannot be created in development football. I therefore believe players need real-life first team experience.

I do not have all the answers to all the questions around these issues, but I will emphasise that every player is different and has a diverse range of personal and professional requirements. One size simply does not fit all, and it frustrates the life out of me when a programme of learning is developed for athletes in which everyone gets the same deal. We're not dealing with school kids here who will sit the same exam at the end of the year. We are dealing with athletes that in a football context have different bodies and minds and play in different positions in differing formations for different leaders and clubs. It's your job as the coach to meet those needs whether they are technical, tactical, physical or psychological. These are the obvious textbook needs, but the player might need help socially or with their family. Who knows?

Most importantly, do you know what your players need?

I urge all coaches, teachers and developers reading this book to think about whether they are going to get their players to take part in the 'three-point football zone' to ensure that they experience an authentic, professional and thought-out reason for doing what they are doing.

To finalise this chapter, I'm going to ask you a question, which is: *What is more important for athletes?*

- Proving yourself in a 'three-point zone' at a lower level?

Or

› Playing in the under 23s/reserves' 'development zone', in a place where there is safety and comfort?

I'll let you decide, but just ensure you are accurate. *(My thanks to Darin Kilpatrick, FA Coach Educator and former Bognor FC manager, for his inspiration in writing this chapter.)*

SECTION TWO
First Half – Teaching Tips

This section of six chapters looks into the nitty-gritty of truly effective teaching and learning techniques, as well as the self-awareness that's needed to implement them. It assesses the growth mindsets of adults, the use of data in schools and performance environments, how to accelerate learning and the best strategies to add value to human performance.

CHAPTER 9

Seven Million is too Many!

The Real Issue About Growth and Fixed Mindset: Not Regarding the Kids, but YES, the Adults!

"From the neck up is where you win or lose the battle. It's the art of war. You have to lock yourself in and strategise your mindset. That's why boxers go to training camps: to shut down the noise and really zone in." – Anthony Joshua

Growth and fixed mindset are the latest buzzwords in the teaching, learning, coaching and educational psychology world. I have been studying Carol Dweck, a leading global educational psychologist, for a decade now, but it's only in recent years she has come to more people's attention. She is a phenomenon in schools, academies and on social media. I believe her two popular buzzwords/terms are used wisely, but they're often misinterpreted, too. Let me explain:

Firstly, constantly telling a human to have a *'growth mindset'* in a vague and flakey way means nothing and will often lead to a failed outcome. All I see over social media these days are pictures and diagrams of this positive way of thinking. I'm at my wits' end about people's misuse and their lack of understanding of the terminology. To be honest, it can cause more harm than good. I've heard many so-called experts use this term, but I sense they do not really understand the concept themselves. My advice is that they need to understand how people succeed and fail in order to fully grasp the term. Simply saying growth mindset over and over again will never be enough to build resilience and provide positive outcomes and add value for people. As an example, we know that children who fail in academia, sport, or otherwise, often do so for a host of reasons.

These could be:

- Lack of confidence in the subject/sport.
- Low aspiration from the coach/teacher or themselves.
- Parents not engaging in the education/coaching/teaching process.
- Uninspiring and fixed or rigid curriculum, leading to boredom for the learner.
- Poor and uninspiring teachers or coaches.
- Struggling to retain information, which often leads to exam failure/poor performance and therefore increased stress from all of the above. And so the negative cycle continues.

I feel confident in saying that many children fail to understand that most adults don't regard themselves as brainy or talented. All young people need to know is that being brainy or talented is rare and does not exist as much as they may think it does. Sadly, in the UK education system, an exam factory culture has been created, which is often cleverly disguised in buildings called schools (note my sarcasm). This means the term brainy is solely linked to, you heard it, how well you do at exams. The British historical phenomenon of exam overkill is ludicrous and often damaging. Any adult reading this knows the importance of qualifications, and their significance in certain work sectors. However, the wise folk among us also know that life's destiny, achievements, successes and outcomes are not always linked to exams or talent. Driving a London taxi is a great career. These people basically do a four-year degree in memory. As far as I am concerned, this is an incredible skill.

Many of you reading this may well disagree with my theory, and assume that success in life is heavily linked to exam results or talent, but hopefully you can still see both sides to this argument. I know for certain that I would not be writing this book had I not learnt the true meaning of growth mindset, developed techniques to believe in my own ability and implemented a high work ethic to become, in later years, a so-called expert. After all, I am still learning, evolving and changing. For the record, if you haven't already read this, during my formal school years I left without a single GCSE to my name.

How many of you reading this did the same?

How many of you walked away from school or a failure in sport demotivated about the learning experience and life's goals and opportunities, and were generally worried for your future? Did you go back to do retakes? Or, if released from the sport you loved, remain in it in another capacity, such as a coach or teacher? My best mate from school, James Morris, was miles more intelligent than me. All I ever did in history lessons was to ask him the answers to most questions. And, as I was a loud mouth, I was not shy about speaking out in class. James was much bigger than me, but he was too shy to answer. He is now a successful floor tiler and builder and could have gone to university with ease. He was just never bothered. But James and I aside, I truly believe that negative school experiences mean that some people become fixed in their mindset and view themselves as unintelligent. They are intelligent, but they just do not think or feel it simply because of how they performed when they were 16 years old and because schools and society labelled them so early. It is completely crazy that British society puts so much pressure on people at such a young age, which then affects them into adulthood. This is a sad and dangerous negative sociological cycle, which exists in Great Britain and beyond.

Are you one of the seven million people living in Great Britain right now who views themselves as unintelligent?

I could easily be in that bracket and have a fixed mind-set towards being unintelligent. But luckily I had parents who told me to re-educate myself and try again by doing retakes. We all know the ability to bounce back from defeat is key in life.

This poisonous and negative trend in education and sport is very common in modern society, and failure is due to many reasons. These are supported by other variables, also linked in examples below:

- Parents who were not educated and so do not value education themselves. (A fixed mindset towards being unintelligent.)

- A child, turned adult, with a poor history and memories of school. When they then become a parent their children also struggled. (A fixed mindset towards being unintelligent.)

However, the problem with modern schools and how in many ways they mimic exam factories, as I have previously mentioned, is that they are failing society. The current design of the curriculum is dated. What goes on in education now simply does not meet the needs of a modern society. It's a similar approach to the sports coaches of many years ago, who for decades assumed that the only way to motivate players and help them achieve was to shout at them. Society has changed. You cannot shout at the youth of today.

Most coaches back in my day were so poor emotionally and intellectually that their only talent was to point out the worst attributes of the players week after week, while assuming it was making them better at the game. Remember that these coaches were the same ones who were selecting the players. They certainly didn't have to pick the ones they went on to tell were rubbish! Incredibly, my mate Steffan Ball did what every player wants to do but rarely has the bottle. In a game for Dulwich Hamlet, he walked out at half time and went home. He hadn't been subbed, he had simply had enough of the manager shouting at him for weeks on end. In his final game for the club, he packed his bags at half time and said to his manager, "You're meant to be my manager, remember, and that means helping me, not contributing to making me worse." It's a great story that one and it makes me laugh every time I think about it.

In my years of studying and applying this research and pedagogy to my work, many theorists have influenced me. But the one who stands out from the crowd is Howard Gardner and his theory of multiple intelligences. In his book *Multiple Intelligences*, he describes seven different types, which all vary greatly. Sadly, the only intelligence that is recognised in Britain, in particular, is the academic one. So, imagine this. You are one of the seven million people who left school at 16 with no formal qualifications to your name. As a result of this time in your life, you believe you're not intelligent and have subsequently struggled with your mindset ever since. But have you ever thought about all the people who struggled to attain those five A to C GCSEs, but possessed the following skills?:

- ✓ Could speak several languages.

- ✓ Had brilliant logical and mathematical skills, and a capacity to learn and problem solve in all areas of life.

- ✓ Had spatial-visual intelligence and the capacity to think in images and pictures, and to visualise accurately and abstractly.

- ✓ Had bodily-kinaesthetic intelligence. For example, being brilliant at sport. They could run, jump and were agile, powerful, strong and quick. They had the skills to build a house, make a cabinet, plumb a house, fly an aeroplane and be an artist, etc.

- ✓ Had musical intelligence – i.e. they could play an instrument superbly.

- ✓ Had interpersonal intelligence and an ability to detect and respond appropriately to the moods, motivations, feelings, emotions and desires of others.

- ✓ Had intrapersonal skills and the ability to be self-aware and in tune with their inner feelings, values, beliefs and thinking processes, and just generally be a good person.

Most people reading this will probably have the fourth tick screaming out at them. Compared to other nations, schools in Britain, on the whole, don't reward pupils for being good at sport. There are always the few that do, and a particular well done to the UK's private schools, which have produced Olympians and whose pupils have achieved success in sports such as rugby, cricket, tennis and rowing. It's a sad situation for the less fortunate athletes, who weren't given the opportunity to flourish using the skills they were born with because they attended schools without such good resources.

What private schools do prove is that it is possible for young people to succeed academically and athletically if they are provided with the right support, intervention and environment. I often think the football industry has low aspirations about the dual pathway. It is well known that young people adapt to challenge and shouldn't be defined by one aspect of their life, because if that doesn't work out they need another pathway. Additionally, the journey in both school and sport can be mutually supportive. Doing your best at school enhances discipline and focus and helps build resilience for those on-the-pitch experiences.

I urge all adults and children to at least try to have a growth mindset and be open minded about changing their thoughts, emotions and behaviours. How many adults do you know who are know-it-alls and will not budge from their opinion because of their own experiences? These types of people can be difficult to deal with, but they need to understand that opinions (on any topics) don't have to always be fixed and rigid. It should be noted that opinions can change, improve and evolve. In basic terms, the meanings of the words resilience, repetition, effort, desire, passion and integrity are key ingredients to any person's success. A thirst to learn new concepts is truly powerful. Most importantly, for the people who struggle to learn effectively, I advise you to Google 'learning to learn' skills. This is another vital cog in the journey to success. This final quote from Gardner summarises everything perfectly:

> "People have different strengths and intelligences. For example, students who are 'interviewed' as a means to gain access to a course may be mislabelled as being less than desirable because of inappropriate assessment (poorly written interview questions, bias toward a perceived 'perfect student', and other narrow criteria).
>
> "In life, we need people who collectively are good at different things. A well-balanced world, and well-balanced organisations and teams, comprise people who possess a different mixture of intelligences.
>
> "This gives that group a fuller collective capacity than a group of identical specialists."

CHAPTER 10

What is Knowledge and Learning for Elite Coaches and Teachers?

"Intelligence shows itself not so much in always having the right answers but in being able to ask the right questions." – Dave Meier

The title of this chapter is fascinating, as I still do not know the answer myself. In my first week of teacher training at university, I heard the following quote and loved it so much that it has stayed with me ever since:

"Tell a player and they will forget.

Show a player and they will remember.

Involve a player and they will understand."

Have you ever thought about the impact of truly effective learning in your working environment, maybe a school, business or sports team?

I'd like you to think about these following questions:

- Who is the most knowledgeable person you work with, and why?
- What is it about their experiences and the information they've retained that makes them so knowledgeable?
- What does their knowledge feel and look like to you?
- How does their knowledge link to better performance for all the people they work with?

For example, regarding elite sportsmen and women, how does the knowledge (good and bad) of the coaches lead to elite performance outcomes, including victories, losses and progression or regression, in actual games over a period of time?

Here is a question that was put to me by Doctor Bob Burstow in my first ever lecture at King's College for my Masters degree. He said:

"How do you know that you know something?"

The whole lecture theatre went silent as one hundred senior educators sat there deep in thought.

"Have you ever thought about that concept?" the professor said. *"Probably not!"* He then added, *"So, I'll ask again. How do you know that you know something?"*

The professor followed on with:

- Did someone tell you?
- Did you learn it for yourself?
- Did you read something?
- Did you experience something for yourself?
- Did you fail at something?
- Did you see something?

And then he said, "How do you know that the person telling and giving you the knowledge, showing you knowledge, involving you and lecturing you is giving you the accurate FACTS?" To all people reading this, I don't want to get all deep on you just a few sentences into this chapter, but here is a word I think you should know. It really has changed my life regarding the subject of *"knowledge"*.

> *"EPISTEMOLOGY"* This simply means: *"The study and theory of knowledge."*

So, the reason this word and meaning is so important in sport and life is because it's likely that the knowledge you have acquired over the years has three actual narratives:

1. Might well be a fact and be correct
2. Might actually be wrong
3. Might be partially correct

Have a think about all of the agreements and disagreements you have had over your lifetime, whether at work, with friends or with family. These differences are normally because of two things. These are either: opinions or facts.

Either way, this opinion or fact attitude is dangerous in any work or team environment, as we know that people in the football industry have an ego. So, before you start arguing your case about team selection or training methodology, ensure that you're talking facts and do not assume everyone else is stupid and clueless. Have a think about the validity and accuracy of what you are saying. Benjamin Franklin was quoted once as saying: "An investment in knowledge pays the best interest."

So, ensuring that your knowledge is accurate is key. I've been around many people in my lifetime that have really strong personalities but are actually pretty stupid. However, because of their strong personalities (I call them unconsciously incompetent and clueless about being clueless), they often get their own way with people. The correct way to discuss sporting decisions and life includes the obvious decision-making processes that need to be implemented, such as: listening to others, sharing ideas, researching potential pros and cons and ensuring the team, business or family has a shared goal on how they move forwards with facts.

So, let me explain some evidence-based knowledge that people in the world once understood as fact, which then became untrue. Society once said the following:

- The world is flat.
- You can only run at peak speed with a high knee lift. (For decades,

athletics books said that to run the fastest you had to sprint with high knees – American Michael Johnson proved that fact to be wrong.)

- In the 1920s, selling cigarettes to hospital patients was accepted and they were told it would not harm their health.
- For decades, footballers ate steak before a game assuming it was the best thing nutritionally they could consume before running onto the pitch.
- Before Roger Bannister's four-minute mile, scientists said that no one could achieve it, as it was physiologically impossible. Now the record time is 3:43.13.
- It's widely said that goldfish have a seven second memory – yet again, that's not the truth.

In some way, shape or form, these 'facts' have been proven wrong. Therefore, wrong knowledge has been invented – almost.

After 20 years (and with my tongue firmly implanted in my cheek), I believe I have a rough idea about the accuracy of the knowledge I have attained in my field of work, but I can honestly say that the failures I have experienced have played a large part in this. They have been powerful moments that have helped me learn and, hopefully, become more knowledgeable.

I am not implying that any single teaching, coaching or leadership strategy is factually the best process to use, but what I am saying is this:

> How do you know that your way is the right strategy to use for your players or the staff in your workplace?

The former England manager, Sven-Goran Eriksson, was one of many who thought England could only play 4-4-2. So, therefore, Paul Scholes, a classy central midfielder, had to play left midfield. In fairness, England played that formation for decades and, therefore, historically, some would say it hindered our flair players for years. Glen Hoddle, in his playing days, is a prime example of someone who got caught up in this nonsense. He was a footballing genius who only acquired 53 caps and should, in my opinion, have been 153! You could therefore assume that 'epistemology flaws' have happened in footballing history. The evolution of tactics and sport science has been so vast that coaches need to ensure their current knowledge is accurate. As I previously described in this chapter, knowledge changes, including sporting knowledge, so you must be careful not to stay fixed in your mindset. What worked then may not work now.

So, in summary, I urge you to become more self-aware about your knowledge so that you get into better habits and become more measured, less emotional and consistently say things that are factual and objective rather than based on opinion. Secondly, try to understand why you are saying what you are saying, how you say it and when you say it. After all, many people in football don't listen – they just talk!

One hugely significant method that has definitely helped me become more fact-orientated when working with elite athletes is how we use technology. Video analysis, in particular, holds no lies. Watching matches on repeat, or observing yourself teach or coach, makes you realise that your initial opinions about what really happened (in that snapshot) were an inaccurate assessment. This process, therefore, helps knowledge become more accurate with: FACTS and not OPINIONS.

Finally, you know you're in a great place with your knowledge when your opinions are facts.

Take heed of this wisdom from Maori tribes: "From listening comes knowledge, from knowledge comes understanding, from understanding comes wisdom, from wisdom comes wellbeing."

CHAPTER 11

The Problem With Teachers

"A good teacher who can take the zero pay and help kids develop physically, emotionally and socially, is literally an angel."
– Eva Amurri

I used to say to my old school colleagues:

"The government are mostly to blame for the current state of education provision, and contribute to the stresses of many teachers across the country. All this bureaucracy, and yet no gain in standards has been achieved."

However, in fairness to all the bureaucracy, I believe if ALL the nation's teachers stood in one line, 70% of them would be described as odd. Michael Gove, the former education secretary, isn't a teacher, but his strange decisions affected their wellbeing and induced symptoms of stress, that's for sure. However, let me tell you (again), teachers really can be a strange bunch. Now, I have been described as odd loads of times, so I can accept this title. However, what's weird about some teachers is that you'd think they would be the most passionate about learning and improving themselves, when, in fact, if they are set a challenge, such as teaching another subject, they just moan and act as if the world has ended. No one can ever take away the passion I've had for learning my trade, upskilling more experienced colleagues and adding value to not only my own repertoire of skills, but in turn to the children and adults that I have served for over two decades. I have taught PE, maths, science, geography and dance to classes for at least a year formally, and sat in every cover lesson imaginable, teaching RS, business and languages … badly, may I add.

At my worst, I'm better than the average teacher. Teaching skills are one thing, but experiences are another and, having taught some children who had quite literally seen their parents murdered in foreign countries before seeking asylum in the UK, it was impossible to not care very much. Teaching was not just a job to me – it was my life, in more ways than one. My brother is a headteacher, my mother is a retired teacher and all my best friends are teachers. A reason they are on my friends list is because they are all exceptional practitioners. I have always said I could never go for a drink with someone I didn't respect or value at work. It is against my teacher morals.

How could I spend a Friday night in the pub with a colleague that has left work early every day, failed to teach good lessons and worked with zero passion?

I would be living a lie if I said I respected anyone who worked like that. I simply don't respect them and essentially I never will, because there are too many of them floating about in the system. Education of any form, and the art of educating people, has been experienced by everyone, whether they are young, old, rich or poor. We all have an opinion on it from our past, don't we? You can surely remember your best ever teacher and why they inspired you. And you can probably remember the worst one, and how they demotivated you.

On reflection, what constitutes a good and bad teacher is highly subjective I suppose. But is it? Ninety-nine per cent of the kids that I have taught in schools could tell me who the best and the worst teachers were in all of the schools I worked in. You simply just had to ask them. They would say things like:

"Sallis, let me explain. Mr Simpson is the best teacher because he's so passionate. Lessons are fun, which makes us more engaged and we learn more."

They might also say things like, "Ms Jones makes learning her subject so enjoyable and she inspires us to be the best we can be. Everyone loves her. As for Mr Marshall, he's a shocking teacher. He doesn't care about us or teach us anything. He can't even control us. Everyone just mucks about." (Apologies if there are any Mr Marshalls out there. These names are merely fictional.)

CHAPTER 11 - THE PROBLEM WITH TEACHERS

So, what is the problem with teachers?

- Some lack passion for the job.
- Some genuinely dislike children's company.
- Some have never failed at anything academic in their life, so they cannot empathise with people and children who do struggle.
- Some could be good, but they are simply working in the wrong type of school, i.e. inner city teaching just doesn't suit them.
- Some younger teachers think quick promotion is their right, even without the necessary experience or expertise.
- Some older teachers are negative and possess a glass half empty mentality.
- Some modern school leaders simply cannot lead to save their life and think it involves spending their time monitoring their staff and filling in tick boxes of what they aren't doing well, instead of focusing on their good points.
- Some moan constantly and simply don't realise how lucky and privileged they are to teach and help our future generations excel.
- Some are simply in the wrong career and perceive their job as something that pays the bills.
- Some are simply unlucky at the start of their career. They may have been mentored poorly by university lecturers or school leaders. Therefore, they get into a mindset of simply 'thinking what they think' and 'knowing what they know' is right ... when they could not be more wrong! Retraining the minds of these staff is tough, to say the least.

So, I have stated the problems quite clearly and not held back, but what about all the outstanding teachers out there? Trust me, there are many. I couldn't list the ones I've had the privilege to work with. However, I believe these experts are being let down by the weaker teachers in the industry.

Alarmingly, the good teachers and the bad teachers get paid exactly the same. And when good teachers start leaving the industry, that's when the government should worry. And unfortunately they are – in abundance.

So:

- ✓ Bad teachers … up your game.
- ✓ Middle leaders … start managing and upskilling the people you serve.
- ✓ Senior leaders … stop the crisis management mentality and show some empathy, kindness and true leadership acumen.
- ✓ Headteachers … start caring more and stop monitoring.
- ✓ And as for the government … sort your lives out and seek the opinions of the experts, not the sheep! How can you have an education secretary that has never been a teacher?

CHAPTER 12

The Importance of 'Adding Value' in Sport

But does it always happen in your team, school or business?

"The single and only aim of any teacher, coach or manager is to improve the people you serve, in every facet of development. You cannot just be judged on promotions, relegations and trophies." – Steve Sallis

I'm proud of the above quote, and I am happy for you to steal it, share it and save it for future use. We often talk to athletes who are involved in elite performance environments about 'controlling the controllables', but what about the coaches following the same process? Coaches at all levels need to get a better understanding of the fact they can only control what they are in charge of. In modern society, we often judge a coach's or teacher's expertise by the end point of the player or learner's development journey.

For example:

- Have they made it professionally after five years at the club academy?
- Did they get an A grade in their maths exam?
- Has an Olympic sprinter achieved gold?
- Did they make a test match debut in cricket after years of potential as a youth athlete?
- Did their team win the league?

Do you feel those questions are fair and justified for the people in charge of an athlete's development, at the various levels they work at? If so, I pose these questions to you:

> Is the manager who wins the premier league with the biggest budget the best manager?

> In contrast to the above question, is a reserve team manager that produces five first-team standard players per season, but fails to win a game all season, a failure as a coach?

Sadly, in both cases, the untrained eye will view both scenarios at face value, without the deeper level of understanding it takes to grasp what true and pure player development is. In October 2017, I joined Hastings United as the Assistant Manager, when they were 19th in the league. Five months later, when I left, we were ninth. We were not good enough for promotion, so all we could do (and all we could control) was to help the players improve. I used to bore them to death by saying, "Get the process right." A coach or manager's career can get tarnished before they have even started, thanks to the short-term mindset the football industry adopts, which includes a lack of understanding from many board members, the media and other people outside the confines of the training ground. This can be catastrophic for the coach in charge, as people who know nothing about football are put in charge of making football-related decisions. I am aware that 70% of the first-time managers in the English Football League who are sacked aren't able to get another job. From experience, this isn't because they know little about football, it is because they know little about everything else that's needed as an elite manager in the modern game. I have always said there is a person behind the player, so understanding people is a priority. And how does one go about understanding people? Go and work in a school! That will test you. Dealing with kids who refuse to do what you tell or ask them to do every 30 seconds isn't easy.

I believe you cannot base your judgement of athletes or people on an academic journey by comparing their achievements. Comparison is not always healthy. Life, education and sport pathways are not always that straightforward. My next statement refers back to my teaching days, and a dissertation I wrote about how to achieve effective learning outcomes for athletes:

> *"Individual athletes or teams should only be graded and assessed on the rates of PROGRESS they have made as an individual or group, and not on the end point. Winning is not possible for everyone. The impact they have had on their own learning journey and how far they have travelled on that journey are the most important aspects to consider."*

An important question to ask when assessing player development is this: *Did anyone monitor or measure the starting point of their learning journey?*

As I mentioned before, when I joined Hastings, we were 19th in the league and subsequently climbed ten places. I would also like to mention that we created the youngest team in the club's history. Therefore, my legacy was to help produce a team that had *growth* rather than a bunch of overpaid names that would go from club to club, season after season. Being able to accurately measure how much progress your learners have made is vital for both them and you. The rocky road of teaching, learning, mentoring and coaching individuals and teams can be hard. Over the years, I have witnessed many people become frustrated by the outcomes of their teams' and players' end points. They feel uneasy and anxious about their lack of success. What I'd like you to do now is think again about what success means for you and the team. Basically, be ridiculously aspirational, but realistic, otherwise you will drive yourself mad. Remember that every team or athlete has a ceiling point, you just need to know where it is and make sure you get them there. When I refer to the outcomes, I mean the end point, whether that be:

- Failure at an exam.
- An opinion on whether the player is good enough/not good enough to make it as a professional footballer.

- A sprinter that came fourth place in an Olympic final and was perceived as having failed.
- Not picking up three points on a Saturday with a victory.

All of the above have a context. Failure and success are both relative.

I would be lying if I said I didn't get frustrated with the talented players I worked closely with who failed to make the grade. But, as I mentioned in Chapter Two, talent is 25% of an athlete's portfolio. So many of you reading this will be emotionally connected to your players, as I have been. I have now left Millwall Football Club, but if any of those players picked up the phone and asked for help, I would be there. The same goes for all my former pupils – all 30,000 of them! I would try to help every single one of them. What are we on this planet for, selfishness or selflessness? Friends often tell me off when we go out to the pub, as nearly every time a former pupil who wants to say hello gives me a nudge. I make it a priority to take time out to chat to them. After all, they have decided to come and speak to their ageing teacher. It's the least I can do and it's also an honour.

Generally though, the athletes whom I mentioned earlier, who didn't fulfil their potential, had let themselves down over the time we had worked together. Often they had the talent but struggled to take on board all of the various technical, tactical, physical, psychological and educational advice and information that highly experienced and supportive staff had given them. They won't be the first or last teenagers to get lazy, of course, and, on balance, not everyone can succeed in sport, business and education. However, everyone CAN make progress and improve!

Over the years, I have come to learn that some educators and coaches have a greater moral conscience than others. Some don't lose any sleep at night, as they know they have done everything within their power to add value to the player or learner they are serving. To put it simply, they are achieving their aim to make them better in life and their chosen sport. Larry McAvoy, Kenny Brown, Seb Barton, Dan Mlinar, and Paul and Dean Palmer are guys who really stand out in professional football. Not only are they football coaches, they are also taxi drivers, mentors and support systems to these players. These guys *truly* care. We so often forget that behind the player is a human being. So when I say the words *add value*, what am I adding value to? My answer is simple:

1. The person
2. The performer/learner/athlete

Adding value also involves correlating and synchronising the two to ensure holistic success.

Simply put, therefore, in order for long-term success to be achieved by the performer, learner or athlete, they have to be a successful person. If not, their career will be destined to fail at some point. Let me give you some context …

> Have the player's schooling and academic grades regressed or progressed in the time they have been with you? Would you even know? Would you even care? Trust me, kids want to know that you care about this aspect of their life development. So, instead of starting your session talking about passing and shooting, start by asking them about their day at school, their favourite lesson or their best teacher. That is truly holistic. If you are the type of person who hated school and saw education as holding no value in your life, that doesn't mean they will be the same.

> Has the athlete's performance got worse or better under your supervision?

> Is the athlete's lack of form and the fact (and as managers often say) they're not 'doing it right now' down to them or you? Are your poor tactics, training methodology and manner of approach making them worse?

If you can answer the questions in detail, then morally you are in a good place as a practitioner. The ex-Brentford, Glasgow Rangers and Nottingham Forest manager, Mark Warburton, has been interviewed many times over the last few years. I regularly hear him use the term 'adding value'. I am sure this type of language usage came from his time working in the City of London, in his previous job as a trader. Many times he has been quoted as saying:

> "Yes, this player will add value to the current group of players we have."

Danny Cowley, the former PE teacher and now Lincoln City manager, also uses the same type of language. Danny went to the same university as me, although he was three years below. There is no doubt that his teaching experiences have made him who he is today. Dave Livermore often says that Danny and I have similar personality traits. I personally wouldn't know, but it's a compliment. The Cowley brothers are a class act, pure and simple. Danny's brother, Nick, is also a PE teacher and I regard both men in the top quality category. As the saying goes, there is no I in team and Nick is also the brains behind the process and has equally contributed to Lincoln City's success. I have watched Danny's first interview as Lincoln City's manager about five times now on YouTube. He oozes knowledge, confidence and class. At one stage, referring to the work ethic in football, he states:

> "I don't know one company in the world that is successful working for two hours a day."

He's basically implying that modern-day athletes and staff have to do more hours in the day in order to succeed, compared with the old-fashioned footballers, who literally did two hours work before going off to the snooker hall or golf club.

Have you ever really thought what the saying adding value means and how it should be interpreted in terms of your role at work? I have regularly interpreted it as the staff helping players and people to achieve by adding value to: "Every single facet of the development process."

CHAPTER 12 - THE IMPORTANCE OF 'ADDING VALUE' IN SPORT

Yes, you heard it – the process. Simply put; just get better. So, what is the process in terms of development for athletes? Is it as simple as playing games on match day? Or, looking at the bigger picture, is it about contributing to all the nuances of what elite teams and athletes need to do?

These include:

- ✓ **Train hard**
- ✓ **Be a good person**
- ✓ **Get better every day**
- ✓ **Work selflessly**
- ✓ **Follow instructions**
- ✓ **Manage yourself to be effective**
- ✓ **Behave well**
- ✓ **Be coachable**, with a growth mindset. In layman's terms, this amounts to being a cohesive part of the performance wheel.

In summary, players should uphold what Dave Brailsford, a big influence of mine, calls CORE values. Dave is the Team Sky cycling team leader.

These values comprise:

- ✓ Commitment
- ✓ Ownership
- ✓ Responsibility
- ✓ Excellence

It has been proven that if you instil this sort of independence and, most importantly, ownership, early on in an athlete's life, they are far more likely to be successful. However, I should mention that by the late teens habits have been formed and we get into the complex development I call unlearning. This will only confuse you, so I won't go there in this chapter.

Helping athletes achieve is a priority for all coaches and teachers. A common educational term called a *'scaffolded learning'* process is a key ingredient for success. This means helping the athlete to 'access and understand' the learning and knowledge you are providing in good detail. Basically, this is vital, and if you achieve this skill in your coaching then you really are adding value. A final example, and something for us all to question, is this scenario:

If your team finishes fourth from the bottom of the league one season and fifth from the bottom the following season, and achieves more points, then, to put it bluntly, you have added value.

However, to throw a curveball into the equation regarding how you should accurately validate success, I will get you to think about this hypothetical question regarding Claudio Ranieri, the Leicester City manager who won the premiership in 2016. Would he have added value following their premier league title-winning season, if in the following season he achieved more points but did not win the league?

Hmmm … tricky question that one. I'll let you decide. It's truly complicated, eh? The subjective nature of sport and the variables of opinions, emotions and outcomes is not always clear-cut.

CHAPTER 13

'Accelerated Learning' and What it Really Means in Football

"Accelerated learning is the single most important new advance in education and self-development." – Brian Tracy

Often in the workplace, people hear terms and phrases that they go on to use but do not always truly understand. However, when these key terms are said over and over again, it genuinely leads to institutional change at work. These phrases then start to become key language in helping remind even the best of coaches and teachers that what they are trying to achieve, put simply, is: **EXCELLENCE**

Fundamentally, accelerated learning is the mechanism to help the people you serve do one thing:

> **Learn faster than the average learning strategy!**

My former colleague, Chris Perry, was a premier league defender who used to pleasantly mock me most days about this term, but when I heard him use it with players during conversations, I knew deep down it was having an impact in some way. I will highlight below my top 10 most effective ways to accelerate learning in an educational organisation.

This could be a:

- Sports club
- School
- Business

The following 10 methods are based on my experiences of learning, which I have used in schools, universities and throughout my years in football to support my peers, including senior leaders, players, academy coaches and teachers.

The 10 methods of learning

1. **Agree with the people in the building about what the key objectives to accelerated learning are.**

    This means that you get buy in from the workforce. That way, all of the staff, including management, are aware of what the Key Performance Indicators (KPIs) are that help embed the learning processes for the learners with greater rigour and detail. This creates more meat to the bone for the athletes. If the managers are not buying into the language and process, why should the rest of the staff? Over the years, when I have conducted teacher-training sessions, I've asked staff to complete surveys on the impact of these strategies. One of the top reasons for learning not sticking has been because there has been no line manager follow-up to address the impact of the learning KPIs.

2. **Ask the learners/players what they want to get out of their own learning journey.**

    Try to meet these targets regularly. If players feel their needs are being met they will engage in the training and, therefore, the learning. Get younger players to write this down in a development diary, otherwise the process becomes too loose. For example, at Millwall, I introduced players presenting to us on a PowerPoint every six weeks, which should be common practice at elite academies these days. Yes, you heard, that is the players presenting and not you! Get them to RAG (Red, Amber, Green) rate whether they feel they have met those targets.

3. **Constantly create variety into your delivery technique.**

    Most of you know this, but to prevent players from getting bored, mix up the weekly routine. Variety will keep the athletes curious. The England rugby team recently boarded their team bus in their kit, only for their coach, Eddie Jones, to take them tenpin bowling instead. Superb!

4. **If classroom based, change pace, movement or tone every 20 minutes.**

    This will keep learners focused and engaged. When you see them switching off, make them stand up and sit down again really quickly. This is an old trick, but one of the best in a classroom setting. So, if you have been presenting new information for 20 minutes, let them have a chance to practice it for the same amount of time. Also allow quiet reflection time for them to take in what they have learnt, as well as lively debates and activities. This also leads to giving learners thinking time once you have delivered a question. My pet hate is not to give someone the time to answer a question. Would this be for your benefit and to make yourself look good with a quick fire, brilliant answer from one learner? What about the rest of the team, who you are letting get away with learning murder? Don't they need to know this content also? Quick answers could be either great or rubbish, but it's key that you ask the questions that will actually get them to think. Kids don't think these days because it's all too easy for them!

5. **Create a positive learning environment.**

    So many teachers and coaches shoot themselves in the foot by saying things like, "This is a bit boring but we need to get through it." I would be lying if I said I hadn't ever said this, but it's better to try and talk to their subconscious and prepare them for a difficult subject using something like, "You will need to focus for this next bit because it will really help you to succeed." This could either be for an exam or to implement their role as a centre forward more effectively. Players get bored with basic passing drills, but how often do they misplace these simple passes? It is also important to emphasise that learning isn't always fun.

6. **Reinforce learning from previous sessions by revisiting it.**

   Often coaches and teachers move to new learning instead of revisiting the current topic. I have noticed how many coaches move onto new tactics when players haven't acquired the previous ones. This drives me mad. For those who know this language, get the 'unit' or 'scheme of work' and throw it in the bin if necessary. Learning is not fixed, so sense and smell the athletes' needs. Ask them how they feel about what is being taught, etc. I believe elite-level coaches do not deliver by coaching out of a textbook. They use their experience and intuition. The textbook is a guide to learning, and it's mostly for beginners.

7. **Dual responsibility and dual buy in.**

   When required, try using a dual contract with the learners and take joint responsibility for what I regularly call the 'learning journey'. As an example, at the start of any two-year programme, it's important to set expectations, targets and, most importantly, monitor those targets. Don't treat your learners like babies but try using these three questions to achieve excellence:

   - In order for this course to help you, it has to be like what?
   - In order for it to be like that, you have to be like what?
   - In order for you to be like that, others have to be like what?

   Get the athletes to deliver the pre-match and post-match team talk. Why not? Don't get sucked into short-termism. So basically, always involve the learner in the journey. The saying below was mentioned in Chapter Ten, but it should serve as a reminder for all.

   > *"Tell a player and they will forget*
   > *Show a player and they will remember*
   > *Involve a player and they will understand."*

8. **Use repetition to make learning stick.**

    Repetition is a vital component to make learning more effective. I often used to test my classes on the same test or exam for up to four weeks. Did I care? No. Was it boring? Probably. Am I strong enough to mentally take the moans and groans? Yes. Does it affect learning and cement knowledge for them? Yes. Is it therefore worthwhile? Yes.

9. **Add building blocks to learning.**

    Start with some small skills and knowledge that they already use and calmly and consistently add to it, which is similar, in a sporting context, to going from 1v1 practices to 2v2, and so on. Often I see learning that is rushed. Let me explain. Effective learning should never be hurried. As an example, when I want young footballers to have more composure and not be rushed in possession, I often get them to imagine having a remote control in their hand with a pause button on it. I get them to think about what it would look like if they pressed the button while they were in possession of the ball. Weird, I appreciate, but it really helps, so my advice is to build pictures with words.

10. **Provide opportunities to use the learning quickly, and use IT.**

    We have all taught a classroom-based session, talked about a science experiment or been involved in long-winded team meetings about how we are going to outwit the opposition. Once done, get them all involved in a practical sense, with the premise, "Stop talking about it and start doing it!" Afterwards, review it. Reflection about current performances is vital, but never rush this process.

CHAPTER 14

The Power and Problem of Performance Data and the C/D Borderline Players

"Not everything that can be counted counts, and not everything that counts can be counted." – Albert Einstein

In my teaching days, there was a huge overload of data. Some of it was good and worthwhile, but most of it was basically pointless. A good friend of mine, and Assistant Principal, Mikey Williams, used to say that the education industry was becoming, "Data rich and system poor." I could see his point. The phrase meant that while we had all this data available to us, we were not using it properly or simply didn't have the time to. Football and elite sport is now pounded with data. Sport scientists, in particular, have it running their programmes in abundance. Some coaches use it wisely, of course, but many use it far too literally. Many tests (in any industry) are valid and legitimate and often measure an objective outcome, i.e. how fast you can run, turn and accelerate. I understand its importance. Data has a massive part to play in the modern development of elite athletes in order to support performance experts. However, as I have said to many colleagues before, "Data should give you as many questions as it does answers."

I urge all aspiring experts to use this philosophy and mindset when it comes to data. It would take a brave practitioner to disagree with those who have worked in education or high-performance environments over many years. Teachers, in particular, deal with spreadsheets comprising 200 pupils, all containing 10 subjects, which include various test scores and data. This is potentially complicated stuff, therefore, the people reading it need to understand that data is there to inform learning and not always to measure it and impact performance. It is certainly not there to judge learning with numbers that link solely to performance outcomes.

In all schools over the years, the second biggest KPI (key performance indicator) behind the year 11 final exam results are the C/D borderline pupils. These are the students at risk of getting the dreaded D grade, but who with hard work, good assessment for learning strategies and rigorous teacher interventions have the potential to achieve one grade higher. The aim to get that infamous C on exam day is what it is all about.

My previous experiences have helped me become crystal clear on how to produce elite athletes. For starters, at full-time elite level, all the staff employed must play an equal part in the development of a programme. This includes coaches, dieticians, strength and conditioning coaches, psychologists, performance lifestyle experts, education officers, physios and kit men, etc. All these stakeholders prevent the below question having any meaning, to be honest:

"Are athletes born or made?"

This question will be talked about forever and a day. I love the question though. So let us look at these made-up analogies as an example:

- The born athletes begin their journey as A-grade students, and they were born with the relevant genetics to be a 100-metre sprinter or have the height of an Olympic high jumper.
- In contrast, the made athletes have a starting point, which is a C grade. Included in this process is the fact that the C-grade athletes still have elements of the physical qualities required for that sport.

So the scenario continues as follows:

- The A-grade (born) performers fulfil all expectations and go on to play in the premier league for 10 years or win a gold medal at the Olympic games, like everyone knew they would.
- The C-grade (made) athletes make it as professional players, but lower down the ladder in League 1. However, they still enjoy a steady career in the game. In an athletics context, the C graders represent their country but without achieving medal recognition. They gain this success by utilising their high levels of intrinsic motivation. We

could possibly say that these athletes have now progressed to a B grade by still achieving a solid career.

The C/D Borderline Players

Now, here are some further questions and metaphors for all you coaches and professionals out there to ponder:

- What about all the athletes that drifted out of the respective sports they were involved in?

Or, in contrast:

- What about the athletes you personally kept in the sport with your expertise, love and passion, which meant you supported them after many wobbles? Well done if you have achieved this.

The C/D borderline players – More about them and the questions you *need* to ask:

- As a coach, have you ever thought about these cohorts deeply enough? (I may be wrong, but after hearing Harry Kane talking recently, I feel he was a C/D borderline player for a long time before he found stardom.)
- Were you a C/D-type player yourself?
- Are these C/D athletes simply not good enough for the required standard, even with all the help available to them?
- Do they fail due to bad luck or being in the wrong place at the wrong time?
- Do they fail because they are poorly coached?
- Have they suffered with injuries, maybe due to dubious medical information? Or were they ignored, as they were not in the top of the group at the time when contracts were renewed?

So, think about athletes at all levels of their chosen sport, particularly the ones who shocked you by ending up getting a professional career when they were perceived as not good enough by the many experts who judged them. These athletes were, at the time of rejection, a D grade. (I think it is important to mention that previous failure somewhere on an athlete's journey may have been a positive experience and the wake-up call they may have needed.) But maybe in contrast, the professional interventions at the time of the D grade were simply not rigorous enough for the athlete.

I have seen this professional neglect for years, with many 14-year-olds being promised the world with four-year contracts, only to get to 18 and be out of the game. Yet again, I pose the questions that needs to be asked about accountability for the failure of these footballers or sportsmen and women. We are qualified adults, remember, so questions linking to our behaviours surely need to include the following:

> - We have the qualifications that claim we are experts. So should we have to act as such?
> - Is the failure of the C/D borderline player their fault or ours?
> - Do some coaches and professional sports people even care about these middle ability players, or just the top end ones? If they don't, they should.
> - Overall, have we done enough holistically for that athlete? Duty of care, etc.

Keep asking yourself the above questions when it comes to the success and failure of the athletes you serve. During my time in the football industry, I have often heard that the player was at fault for not making a career. Is this right or wrong?

Think about the following:

- Is it the player's fault that clubs and the institutionalised culture of football is substandard and akin to pub mentality instead of elite?
- Is it the player's fault that staff members often don't have the skills and empathy to care enough about them to enable them to succeed?

- Is it the player's fault that they are young and coaches hold grudges? (Yes, holding grudges against a child!)
- Is it the player's fault that they do not know how to improve, or have people around them that truly understand all of the above?

I do not claim to know all the answers to all the problems in this chapter, but I do urge you all to think about the C/D borderline athletes. In my opinion, they are the ones that really define a coach's expertise. After all, the A-grade athletes were often born that way (within reason, of course).

Therefore, the real money shot for coaches is getting the athletes that would traditionally be let go from the sport and 'making' them into a success with a list of variables, which include: aspiration, inspiration and rigour of technical, tactical, psychological and physical detail, as well as a programme that really is elite. And when you retire, you really can sit in that armchair, smile and say to yourself as an expert, *"I did everything!"*

Taken together, I believe the human mind and body can achieve anything, and often the C/D athletes have great attitudes, but they just do not know what success looks like or how it should feel. So, in summary, use Carol Dweck's growth mindset approach and further research about top coaching and teaching methodology. By doing these things, who knows what the outcomes could be? Remember the Pygmalion effect as a key driver to success for all athletes? I swear by it! Clifford Stoll once said,

> *"Data is not information, information is not knowledge, knowledge is not understanding, understanding is not wisdom."*

I believe people need to be able to understand in greater detail, in order to really do!

SECTION THREE
Half Time – Coaching Champions

This section of nine chapters focuses on the details of a coach's persona and the importance of subject knowledge. It also examines a coach's philosophy and looks into football leadership, along with how to improve the mindset.

CHAPTER 15

The Singer Not the Song

"There are educated people that are not intelligent, and intelligent people that are not educated." – Steve Sallis

Have you ever known personally or professionally any of the following?:

- A truly great coach
- A great teacher
- A great mentor
- A great friend

Of course you have. Now, think about why the people in these categories have had a lasting effect on your memory? On the flip side, can you remember your worst ever teacher, coach or someone who was plainly clueless? Of course you can.

Have a think about the following questions:

> In your opinion, does gaining a certain qualification mean you are going to be effective at your job?

> How many coaches and teachers do you know who have the top coaching licence or teaching degree?

> What prevents one of these experts from being more effective than the other?

> Have you ever thought about why some coaches/teachers are more effective than others?

> Where and how do YOU compare your skills to theirs?

In the education, leadership and psychology world, we often talk about four categories of people:

1. Consciously competent people
2. Consciously incompetent people
3. Unconsciously competent people
4. Unconsciously incompetent people

Where do you or your colleagues fit into these categories? Now, the title of this chapter is, *The Singer Not The Song*. So, what I am trying to emphasise is the following:

- A qualification (badge of honour) is only as good as the person that uses it properly. Doctor Jacob Naish, a good friend of mine who used to work at Fulham FC Foundation before relocating to Denmark and working for FC Nordsjaelland, is a wise and thoughtful guy. He always says to me when we meet, "Sallis, intelligence, my friend, is not about having a qualification and should not be defined as such. Intelligence is about people's behaviours."

Jacob is right, of course, and to add to this way of thinking, I've come up with three areas where your behaviour is key.

These are:

- ✓ How you act around people (both verbally and non-verbally)
- ✓ How you interact with people
- ✓ How you react to people

Qualifications do not help the above process, but self-awareness does. Therefore, qualifications should support a career and the people they serve, but they should not always be relied upon. Far too often people with qualifications think what it says on a piece of paper is enough to influence others. I can safely say that it truly isn't. Now, I could explain the initial four categories of people to you, but surely with some thought you can work them out yourself. What I will say is that the bottom category is a very dangerous place to be if you regard yourself as a professional, and this applies to any industry – not just sport. Basically, I call these people 'clueless about being clueless'. These individuals are tough to deal with and I have witnessed many of these unconsciously incompetent people cause havoc in the workplace, especially schools and football clubs.

To make matters worse, on many occasions, these unconsciously incompetent folk had first-class degrees from the top universities in the land. These, apparently, proved that they were suitable for the job they turned up at each day. Now, I have worked with some teaching assistants who, although regarded by many as bottom of the pecking order in a school hierarchy, were highly skilled at working with young people and often achieved greater outcomes than anyone else in the system. This is why the title of this chapter is so relevant. I have also always said that a builder with charisma would get more out of a Year 11 bottom set than some fresh university graduate who is way off the mark socially. Teaching, coaching and educating people requires passion, extrovertism and the 'X factor' traits that inspire, not freaky, over educated robots. People that cannot apply their intelligence are fraudsters.

So, before you prejudge people in this society regarding qualifications, think about the skills of the people around you. They may not have a piece of paper that says they are qualified, but think about how they can fit into your institution somehow. However, I do know it's favourable to employ people who have both the qualifications and the skills/behaviours required to do the job well. But, as I've mentioned before, I get extremely frustrated about the obsession with qualifications in our culture. Let me remind you:

"Skills and intelligence should be defined by someone's actions and behaviours, not a qualification."

Think about all the poor quality doctors, teachers and coaches who have exactly the same qualifications as the good ones. Sad, eh? This is the craziest part of our society, and why so many people get away with being ineffective.

As the saying goes:

> "There are educated people that are not intelligent and intelligent people that are not educated."

Which one are *you*?

CHAPTER 16

The Maverick Coach

"I personally believe mavericks are people who write their own rulebook. They are the ones who act first and talk later. They are fiercely independent thinkers who know how to fight the lizard brain. I don't believe many are born, rather they are products of an environment, or their experiences." – Ziad K Abdelnour

We have all known a maverick, whether they are a coach, player or teacher. Sometimes they have been our peers and sometimes they have been our bosses or the people we have managed. If you are not sure of the meaning of the word, the definition is this: **An unorthodox or independent-minded person.**

I love this description, because if you had asked me to define it before I did my research, I would have struggled. What are your thoughts on mavericks? Are they innovators before their time, or simply too emotional and off-the-cuff for your liking? There is a famous saying that goes, "Surround yourself with people who get it." I like this quote and believe it to be helpful. So, do you surround yourself with maverick people or ones with more consistent traits? Do you think you can have too many mavericks in one place?

As a child, I was brought up around many footballers. Many were ex-Brighton players who were mates with my dad from the squash club in Hove. One player who stands out is a man I spent hours and hours with. His name is Teddy Maybank and he's a former Brighton, Chelsea and Fulham player who moved to Brighton for his football career in the late 1970s. I love him like a dad and have watched him throw his golf clubs in anger and laughter on most courses that we've played on. He is a very funny guy and he's one of those larger-than-life characters. Teddy also has many maverick tendencies. Having a maverick in your extended family can be hard to handle sometimes, but when it comes to the various people you work with and with whom you try and achieve goals and aspirations, I believe you have to be likeminded in order to achieve success. The professional and personal boundary is always a fine line, so it's key to ensure that mavericks don't turn professional goals into personal battles. I have seen this happen time and again and it drains the energy levels of everyone.

So, if we look at leadership mavericks throughout modern history, we can assess whether we think their leadership style was effective. The highly successful football manager, Brian Clough, has been lauded for his quirky management style, and he gained much success from it. Arsene Wenger entered British football 20 years ago and, with his teacher-like mannerisms, was certainly different. He could be viewed as an educated maverick. He was certainly unorthodox, but in a good way. Jose Mourinho came onto UK television screens in 2004, telling everyone in the media he was the 'special one'. He would have looked pretty stupid if years later he had not backed up that statement with trophies, but he did. So, what traits do these successful men possess that so many others don't? And how have they created sustained success?

I personally call these gentlemen human psychologists, but without the badge of honour that is a psychology qualification. Their understanding of social science is unbelievable. And, not only are these men highly successful football managers, many people forget that they also all speak around three other languages. That alone is an incredible achievement in life. I would love to speak another language and I personally regard and respect that quality in a person. Have you ever thought about how hard it would be to speak so fluently in different languages and how different these manager's minds and experiences must be compared to the average football coach? When I say minds, I'm trying to emphasise that the main ability and quality of these mavericks is that they think differently to the average manager or coach. They think outside the box, as they say. This lot don't, however, have a box – they threw it away years ago. After all, football is football; it hasn't changed for decades. At the end of the day, it is 11 players against 11 players. I therefore believe that these managers have more creative and agile minds compared to their rivals. And this really was the passion behind my business. I know I can change people's thinking about life and their work and make them understand themselves and concepts better. To do that, I am aware that I also have to think differently. Consider what I am saying here. Doing things differently only happens if you think about things in the first place. This is called metacognition. For these maverick managers to become conventional in their behaviours would be almost impossible. Their idea of being conventional is actually being unconventional on a daily basis. Sometimes these types of people are difficult to predict, but I will acknowledge that it is a lot easier to be a maverick leader when you have had success and a proven track record to back it up, whether that be in sport or business. If you looked at all the highly successful managers who portray maverick traits and attempted to explain a simple ongoing trend in their behaviours, you would possibly put them in the choleric/sanguine corner of Hans Eysenck's *model of personality spectrum*, which dates back to 1947. (Eysenck was a world-leading psychologist specialising in personality and intelligence.) *Which area do you sit in?*

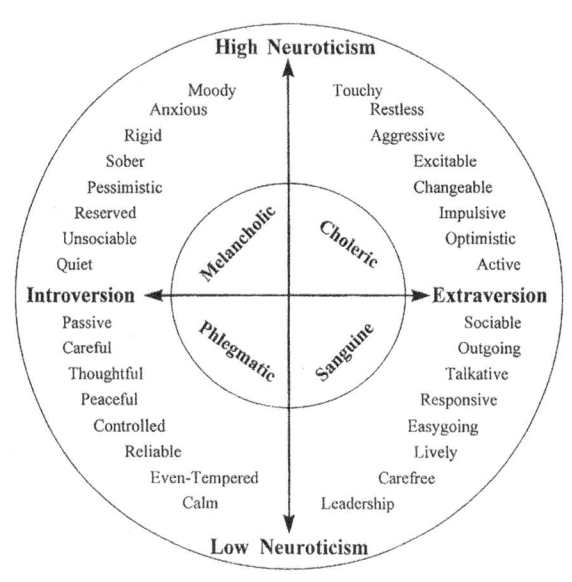

Figure 1. Hans Eysenck's Model of Personality

The maverick teachers I worked with in the past were often mismanaged because they didn't conform to the norms of the tight and rigid school rules. They would gain many plaudits from kids and parents, and would often even achieve great exam results for their classes, but senior managers sometimes simply couldn't handle their personalities and behaviours. My opinion about managing these people is that you have to let them breathe; it's not always the maverick who needs to adapt, but those in charge of them! Sometimes the mavericks I knew were pushed out due to their quirky behaviours.

What is the correct way to approach mavericks when these situations occur?

I'm not always sure, but what I do know is that the two best teaching mavericks I have ever witnessed were Pete Nicholls, a mathematician, and Steffan Ball, a PE teacher. I actually worked with Pete in three schools, so I have a genuine ability to judge. I was with Steffan in two, but we also lived together after university, and he is probably the maddest, funniest bloke I have ever met.

Why were they both so effective?

Pete did everything against the norm, but he was a bloody good bloke. He got great results year after year. The kids also loved him. It was therefore a win-win situation. He was sometimes a nightmare to manage in terms of following the school rules, and his pupils were normally the worst dressed in terms of uniform, which completely contradicted the school's ethos. I spent a lot of my time covering his arse. In our second school together, I had to convince the senior staff to ignore that part of his maverick repertoire. Steffan, a fellow PE teacher, easily got some of the best outcomes for the kids that I ever witnessed during my time in education. He had a completely alternative approach and oozed charisma. How did he achieve excellence? Trust me, you would not put it in a book about teaching and learning. He was the most random character, but he was also the best. It's also important to remember that we were in south London. The kids were characters themselves, so they needed characters teaching them and staff with the skills to handle them. I have always used the phrase 'lively' for how the pupils behaved, so make of that what you will.

I will now give you a simple methodology for managing a maverick. Simply remind yourself of what they do well instead of what they don't do well. Additionally, when dealing with human behaviour, I have always used the acronym A.P.I.

Do you:

- **A**cknowledge their poor behaviours?
- **P**unish their poor behaviours?
- **I**gnore their poor behaviours?

This type of mindset towards leading a maverick is key, otherwise I advise you not to have them in the building or a team in the first place, or else they will drive you mad. I suppose this is similar to managing the flair player in sport. Over the years, cricket is a sport that has had its fair share of mavericks. Kevin Pietersen is a prime example. Additionally, you don't sign the famous former player and French talisman David Ginola if you expect him to defend 1v1 for an entire game.

Can you afford to have someone that is a little bit different but has a sporting 'X factor'?

Whether you are a manager, coach, peer or player, I will let you reflect on your actions. But my advice to you is this. You cannot have enough of them, but only if they are willing to conform! These maverick people are innovators and achieve excellence, just not how you would want it done!

CHAPTER 17

"He Can't Do That!" The Coach Mindset Phenomenon

"Toxic people defy logic. Some are blissfully unaware of the negative impact they have on those around them, and others seem to derive satisfaction from creating chaos and pushing other people's buttons." – Travis Bradbury

If I had £1 for every time I heard a coach say, *"He can't do that"*, I would be a millionaire, Rodney! Since starting in the professional football industry, I have been fortunate to work with some very special people with high skillsets. My 20-year gap, from when I played as a youngster at Brighton, meant that with the benefit of hindsight, I expected a more thorough and rounded approach from the coaches compared to the ones that had coached me. When I entered the role at Millwall, the standard was fortunately miles ahead of where it had been two decades earlier, but in general I am still surprised by the mentality of the coaches at all levels of youth development, and their lack of awareness about their role compared to many of the teachers I had worked with. As Gary Curneen was quoted as saying, *"Youth coaches should always stress the importance of school. An education will take most players a lot further than a great first touch."*

Fortunately, elite and amateur coaching is changing for the better, with teaching and learning at the forefront of coaching pedagogy in the modern world. However, critically, we are still 20 years behind some other nations, but the gap is definitely getting narrower, so well done to all the strategists at the Football Association who have helped make this happen, as well as accelerating learning for us all. The English national team and the social culture that surrounds it realises that we have to rethink our policies on how to achieve greatness. The year 2017 was a magnificent one for the national youth teams, with Euro and World Cup success for many of them. As an example, the feedback I have received from peers about the Football Association Youth Award qualifications has been very complimentary. They are highly focused on child development and educational psychology, which is superb. This toolbox of knowledge can only help in upskilling coaches across the country to reflect on their current practice and seek this knowledge to further inform their future practical and theoretical skills. This will obviously improve coaching performance across all clubs at all levels, with genuine enhanced expertise that comes from years of research about 'how we learn' rather than opinions-based 'what we learn'. The next challenge is that hopefully this knowledge will be implemented and applied to practice on the grass, and therefore add value to the clarity of the 'learning journey' for players and teams. However, cutting to the chase using my experiences, the difference between schools and elite sporting academies is that, in the main, schools do not get to choose the children they get through the door for a five-year period. On the other hand, elite academies get to handpick their athletes. This is the same for all sports, including: tennis, rugby, football and cricket, but the full list is vast. My point, therefore, is hugely significant. In schools, teachers cannot afford to have a mindset that amounts to, "He can't do that!" Quite simply, they do not get a choice, so dismissing students as not good enough, and labelling them early on as not up to the required standard isn't possible. (While I have witnessed this in football many times, it's often because the coach lacks expertise and experience.) When it comes to what's happening in schools, teachers are under greater scrutiny to perform than ever before and feel they have to make the students learn and progress. They have very little choice, which means they have to be more creative when it comes to their teaching style. Jobs are being lost and the British government, which stupidly adopts crazy bureaucratic nonsense, doesn't really care. Teachers have little choice when it comes to acquiring and developing a mindset that innovates, creates and ensures the child makes progress at every level of every subject. It is simply non-negotiable. The teacher's mindset has to be: "This child will and has to succeed over a five-year period of schooling, otherwise I'm gone!" Sadly, no human being should lose their job for an underachieving pupil not pulling their weight. But sometimes, the reality is that the teacher is the reason why the pupils are underachieving, so they have to take responsibility.

The phrase *"he/she can't do that"* isn't in the mental or verbal repertoire of any teacher. Well, it certainly wasn't in the lexicon of any teachers whom I recall as being the best of the best. Football clubs and the industry in general have players who come and go as if on a merry-go-round. I am not saying this has to stop, or that I have all the answers about replacing players, but what I am saying is that the football industry is the only place I know where clubs handpick every single player and then moan about them. As previously stated, schools don't get a choice over who comes through the door – they have to work with what they have got. So my advice to football coaches is: Look at yourself before you start with the blame game. You chose them, so you make them better!

I am not for a minute comparing schools and elite sports academies, as they are not equal in purpose or approach; one is naturally inclusive and takes learners from all walks of life, while the other is exclusive and handpicks athletes. However, in my experience, schools understand teaching and learning at such a greater level that they are able to turn water into wine at a faster pace than the average football coach. In fairness, though, I genuinely believe that coaching has improved in the UK over the last five years. For this reason, my words are not intended to undermine the industry, just merely to emphasise there is still work to do.

To give an example, I'd like to revisit my 'maths man', Pete Nicholls. As previously mentioned, we worked together at three separate schools, which is unheard of in the teaching industry. We went on a great, shared journey as we worked alongside each other in three of London's toughest educational environments. Personality wise, we were like chalk and cheese. I'm louder, opinionated and was more dynamic when fights took place in the corridor. Pete is passive, calm, fun and quite simply a teaching genius. He would regularly inherit 30 lively pupils, who were all expected to fail by not achieving the utopian C grade following a two-year GCSE course. But year after year, school after school, Pete managed to add substantial value to nearly all of the students he served and help them gain that previously elusive grade. Some even gained an A or B! To clarify, this was after they had been predicted to get an E, F or G. Feel free to reflect on how Pete managed to achieve this, but I witnessed it time and time again. This wasn't just about Pete and his maths talents. All around the world there are great teachers in all subjects. Pete was simply a genius when it came to teaching in front of Britain's most deprived and poorly behaved pupils. How professional football academies differ is that the athletes are handpicked for their talents by the clubs. So, if over time these athletes often regress and fail to fulfil their expected outcomes, you should ask these very basic questions:

- What on earth has happened to this player, who for many years was on track to achieve?
- Who is at fault for the failure? The teenager, adult or both?

I have my own ideas, of course, and let me tell you that more often than not the fault doesn't lie with the athlete. I'd also like to remind you that the athlete we are talking about here is a child. Educating a young person so they have good habits is far easier than doing the same for an adult, especially if they are mentored and nurtured properly. Research tells us that in sporting terms, most humans with the correct genetics can cognitively become more intelligent or physically enhance their skill acquisition levels, thus eventually becoming good enough to reach elite levels in certain sports.

As a former PE teacher, the talent ID perspective is fascinating, and when you see a particular ability in a child, you have to establish which sport it is suited to. I therefore believe you have to witness a lot of different sports. I certainly have, and these have made me understand football development better. I took great pride in seeing one former pupil of mine accidentally throw a discus across a playground and through the classroom window of our school. Eight years on, he was a European junior discus bronze medallist!

"He can't do that" is probably allowable in the context of a 100-metre Olympic final, as it is probably genetically out of the question for most of

us, but other sporting achievements are possible with the right coaching and support. In summary, practising anything for half an hour a week will never be enough for world-class outcomes, and this includes maths, playing the violin or a sport. The solutions for success are relentless attention to detail when it comes to the learning journey, coupled with assessment for learning, which is explained in Chapter 26. When these are in place, you will suddenly stop hearing, *"He/she can't do that."*

CHAPTER 18

Teacher or Coach? What Are You? Are Coaches Missing a Trick?

"In the end, it's about the teaching, and what I always loved about coaching was the practices. Not the games, not the tournaments, not the alumni stuff. But teaching the players during practice was what coaching was all about to me." – John Wooden

Over my lifetime as a player, teacher and coach, I have witnessed many bad practices, and this is my resulting advice:

- Stop obsessing in front of your athletes about what they cannot do both technically and tactically. Remind them daily of what they can do and are good at.
- At parent's evenings, stop answering all those super important questions on behalf of your child or cohort of athletes. Let them speak without YOU stopping them in their flow!
- Most importantly, after they have failed at something, ask them, "How does it feel?"

In summary, a top tip to all people involved in development of any age; stop interrupting your athletes when they're talking and let them answer for themselves and this is why I still believe that teaching and coaching practises are flawed in many areas. In a research project, I defined the differences as:

"Coaching often includes motivating and developing a person's skillset in a sport or team setting, and often uses rote learning. Teaching is based on developing and inspiring minds in a structured and innovative way, with a focus on developing a deeper understanding of learning, where emotions connect learning more coherently."

This mainly includes asking questions, such as:

- Why do you do it this way?
- How does it feel when you perform that skill?

I believe there is a key difference and a genuine divide between teaching and coaching methodology. They are thankfully now getting closer, but there is still lots of work to do around understanding these concepts, which need to be promoted in coaching development courses. The obsession with learning always having to be clean-cut drives me mad. Life isn't clean and often neither is learning. The peer pressure amongst adult coaches means the 'look at me' and 'look at how good I am' approach often devalues the outcomes for athletes, as the ego has effectively taken over.

Again, before people think I am condemning coaching, I am not. To support my argument, let me tell you a story about teachers. Over the past 20 years, I have formally and informally observed over 1000 teachers. The subject the teachers taught was irrelevant, because I uncovered many common trends in performance. During my research on effective questioning, the simplified results were as follows:

- The questions the teachers asked the pupils were normally fantastic.

But

- How they delivered the questions to meet the needs of all learners was really very poor.

Reread this again to absorb my point, and have a think about what I have said.

Why deliver these great questions if:

- You are going to answer for the kid anyway? My advice is to let them finish! This type of teacher behaviour materialises all the time. In 2011, I made a note of each time it happened, and discovered that it takes place 75% of the time!
- You let the questions be wasted on a few. Unless all the learners are going to benefit from it, don't ask it.

My advice:

- ✓ Be brave enough to enjoy the awkward silence after delivering a question.
- ✓ Give the athlete/student thinking time after you have delivered the question. (Not in cold weather if you are outside, as keeping them moving is a priority.)
- ✓ If the question you deliver is that important and you require effective learning to take place, then surely thinking time is healthy instead of you giving yourself a false pat on the back for the following scenario: One kid out of a class of 30 answers the question really, really well, and in more depth than you could possibly imagine. You, their coach/teacher, then swiftly moves on in your session/lesson thinking you are the bees knees because one learner out of 30 answered one question. Let me tell you, that's not teaching!

My question is: What about the rest of the group that:

- Has not had to THINK, because you haven't enforced them to do so?
- Has not had a chance to collaborate with a friend or share ideas about the question? (A reminder: the outcome/end point isn't always important in order for effective learning to take place. It is the opinions, good or bad, that challenge learners, so create higher order thinking techniques that stretch and challenge all those you serve.)
- Has not had to brainstorm thoughts, emotions or ideas about anything (because you haven't let them) and has therefore got out of learning jail, because, as I mentioned earlier, one team/class mate has answered perfectly, meaning 29 others don't have to.

So, after reading this, how do you know what the learners know if you fail to ask questions properly and effectively? Trying to gage and measure progress with different types of strategies is key for progress. It is often not the question itself that is the issue, it's how you deliver it. So my advice about effective questioning is to follow the below process with a well-known teaching strategy called *'Think, Pair Share, Square'*:

- Start by connecting the emotions of the learners with the learning that you want them to achieve. So deliver the question with complete clarity.
- Thinking time is then paramount for the learners. I advise a time limit of 20 seconds up to one minute of personal reflective silence after the question has been delivered.
- All learners then have time alone to absorb the question.
- Now pair share the question, allowing pupils to discuss it with a fellow pupil. This helps all learners access the question with a partner.
- Now square it, with the pairs now going into fours.

This is just one example of effective questioning. It hits nearly all assessment strategies: self-assessment, peer assessment and teacher assessment. 1s then 2s and finally 4s (square).

Just think, pair share, square.

CHAPTER 19

Stop Interrupting! Let Them Finish

Team Dynamics Killed in an Instant!

*"If you interrupt someone once, you're not listening.
If you're not listening, you're not engaging.
If you're not engaging, you're not learning." – Steve Sallis*

I used to work with a teacher who interrupted people all the time – staff and kids included. He would drive me crazy when we used to 'team teach' together, as he was so unaware of his behaviour. He would ask the students questions in class and then talk straight over them while they were mid-sentence. This was proper bloody annoying. I remember seeing the look of frustration on the students' faces when he did this. For obvious reasons, he acted the same way during staff meetings, only this time his fellow teachers were sharp enough to address his complete lack of self-awareness … much to his embarrassment. Is this what you do when you are working, coaching or teaching? I am certain that you have at least worked with these people. They never let you finish your sentence, constantly interrupt and never notice how they are behaving. They don't teach this for the UEFA A Licence, do they? Well they should, as the football world also loves an interrupter!

To put it simply, I've placed these people into three categories:

1. **The person who simply isn't listening to anything you say.**

    Depressing, right? Why do I say it so bluntly? Because if they were actually listening to you they would either:

- Let you finish.
- Acknowledge what you've said instead of you basically being white noise.
- Not interrupt you mid-sentence time after time.

2. **The person is listening to what you say, but interrupts you anyway.**

    These people possibly are listening, but because they are so keen to get their point and opinion across, they let their emotions take over and rudely interrupt or talk over you. Again, this is another sign that they're probably not really listening to what you say. We have all been there and it doesn't feel very nice to be on the receiving end of it. It can devalue a relationship in seconds and it happens often.

3. **The person is a loud mouth and their personality overpowers you all.**

    These people are funny. They are the ones who believe that talking louder than everyone else in the room makes them more worthy and correct during a debate. They can be very overpowering and emotional. They tend to lack self-awareness but are often influential because of their strong and often charismatic personalities. However, a sharper, shrewder and more confident individual, who is willing to let them know the impact of their constant interruptions, can soon put them in their place.

So, in summary, if you are going to interrupt people (because we all do from time to time), simply say:

> *"Sorry to interrupt you in your flow, but ..."*

This is a simple, less clinical, softer and more polite way of behaving, which will make you look like an expert listener.

Team Teaching

If you have ever been part of team teaching or coached in partnership with someone, my advice is to get to grips with the synchronicity between the two of you. It is vital you do this, and it's also essential to understand how you can appear to be an amateur in a matter of seconds. At one point, Jimmy Bullard and I got to a stage where we were like an Olympic gymnastics team and everything flowed between us. Speaking over your colleague without acknowledging the interruption is a big no-no. It lacks professionalism and kills respect. Finally, on my return from my first England camp, the staff at Millwall asked me what it was like. I replied in a very straightforward way, *"The knowledge about football and elite development was exceptional, but in my opinion, it was no better than the club down the road or various nations from afar. What was significantly evident was that the England staff were the best listeners I have ever worked with in my entire life."*

Less is more, as they say in the educational world. This experience of 'top level listening' from the England staff during my time at St George's Park, the home of English football, was the best I had ever witnessed. Make of that what you will.

CHAPTER 20

The Half-Time Team Talk: Time to be a Teacher!

The Magic 15 Minutes

"We have to fight, we owe something to the supporters. Don't let your heads drop. We are Liverpool. You are playing for Liverpool. Don't forget that. You have to hold your heads high for the supporters. You cannot call yourselves Liverpool players with your heads down. We have worked so hard to be here, beaten so many good teams. Fight for 45 minutes. If we score, we are in it. If you believe we can do it, we can do it. Give yourselves the chance to be heroes." – Rafa Benitez, 2005, at 3-0 down versus AC Milan

The above match was maybe one of the greatest comebacks in footballing history. Liverpool came from a 3-0 half-time deficit to beat AC Milan and win the 2005 UEFA Champions League. As athletes, we have all been in a losing half-time position. During my playing career, as a child in the 1980s, a teenager in the 1990s, and a non-league player in the 2000s, I would often sit in the changing room at half time and be on the receiving end of the famous 'hairdryer treatment' from various non-league managers. I am certain there were a few occasions when my teammates and I genuinely deserved that type of aggressive treatment. But I would like to emphasise that it was only a few occasions! We all need a rollicking and a telling off on occasion in sport or at the workplace, in order to remind us of the standards required to win a football match or perform better in the office. The problem was that most of us received it every week from our managers – win or lose! They didn't employ any other strategy to interact with us.

In football terms, back in my day, it was also easier to assess a game tactically from the coach's perspective, as there were 1v1 battles all over the pitch. What I mean is, nearly every team I ever played for and against pretty much played a 4-4-2 formation. Young players reading this might laugh, as nearly every opponent plays different tactically these days. However, that rarely happened until after the UEFA European Football Championship was held in England in 1996. Suddenly, professional and non-league teams alike adopted a 3-5-2 formation, which was the one used by the England manager, Terry Venables. Similar processes happened when Jose Mourinho turned up at Chelsea in 2004, and the 4-3-3 formation arrived.

So, why do so many football managers still spend the entire 15 minutes of half time shouting about the problems of the previous half?

Surely it does not take a rocket scientist or for you to read this book to understand how pointless this process of management ranting is. I have many non-league football stories and a few professional ones about this type of behaviour from coaches and managers. I suppose when I joined professional football, I thought there would be a difference between professional, non-league and even Sunday league environments. I often think about the great managers and coaches in different sports, such as hockey, cricket, rugby and basketball, and why there is a different cultural mindset in other sports compared to football. The social demographics are one obvious difference, but maybe there are some other factors that explain why England has won the Rugby World Cup but not the football one.

I often ask myself: Is it just football that attracts a stupid, overemotional and subjective mentality from its managers?

I remember a non-league game that I played with my great friend, Danny Whelan. At half time, our manager verbally abused Danny and spouted all sorts of aggressive nonsense. We were 2-0 down, and to give this story greater context in terms of the fine lines in sport, we were losing to:

- A deflected shot that was hitting the corner flag.

And

- An individual error and moment of madness from our full back.

CHAPTER 20 - THE HALF-TIME TEAM TALK: TIME TO BE A TEACHER!

As a result, as is the case in many matches, there genuinely wasn't much to choose between the teams apart from those two split-second moments. The game had been quite even throughout. I even remember our centre forward missing a great chance in the 44th minute, when he missed an open goal. At half time, however, the manager in question made the biggest and most common error in managerial history, and the telling off became personal towards Danny. He had really crossed the boundaries in the manager/player relationship. Not all players are the same psychologically, of course, and I have heard some players say they prefer a good, old-fashioned manager rant to get them motivated. I personally believe that it has a time and place, but ask yourself this:

> *Are ranting, swearing and shouting still the best ways to motivate players in the modern game, especially considering the different society we have now?*

I personally really doubt it. Young players are different these days. The team talks where you hear 50 swear words in 15 minutes and receive abuse from the manager are long gone, surely? Often, the typical process these ineffective managers follow at half time is:

- Players are shouted at with generic nonsense.
- Players are given no specific feedback about how to improve from a poor half.
- Players hear lots of white noise, about which my mate Danny Lee would say, "By screaming and shouting, all the manager is really doing is motivating himself."

Additionally, every statement made by these managers is normally just vague and lacking any genuine clarity and direction. You often hear things like:

- *"Come on, we need to do better."* (I'd say, "OK, by doing what exactly?")

- *"You lot have been crap."* (I'd say, "OK, why and how have we been crap?")
- *"You need to perform better."* (I'd say, "OK, how do we do that, give us some specifics?")
- *"They want it more than you."* (I'd say, "Because they shout more?")

So, to get back to my original story, after an ear bashing, Danny and I walked out for the start of the second half. Our mood was down, as we really cared about getting the result and changing the 0-2 score. However, on this occasion, we also couldn't stop giggling and mocking our manager. He had just abused us for 15-minutes with what I call 'verbal carnage', and this was for about the fifth week running. The referee even had a laugh with us during the restart, as he said he had heard the abuse we'd received from his changing room next door. What happened next is a moment I will never forget. As Danny was rolling his foot over the ball awaiting the referee's second-half whistle, I said to him in a sarcastic tone, "By the way, mate, what did the gaffer say we have to do to win this game? Any actual tips for us?"

> *Danny replied with a chuckle, "I don't know, mate, I haven't got a clue, but apparently we are all wankers though!"*

As we walked back into the changing room at the end of the game after a 4-1 defeat, the mood was still down. We had performed poorly, of course, no argument there, but we had been led by someone who simply couldn't manage. Our gaffer had no people skills, no strategy, no plan and no understanding of his own behaviour, let alone ours. After some minutes of silence it was time for his post-game feedback and, alarmingly, he went for the jugular and attacked Danny again with more abuse. Danny responded quickly and sharply this time with his own version of events. He quite rightly said: "Well, you're the one who keeps picking me every week and all you do is slag me off. If you don't rate me, either don't pick me or help me perform better. That's your bloody job, isn't it?"

So, in summary, if you are a coach at any level of sport, please remember:

- Half time is for providing solutions to the situation, not for going over the current problems. These problems can be discussed and aired at the end of the game, at the next training session, over a cuppa watching the video back, or one-to-one on the phone, in order to make them more specific and personal to the player or 'position specific units' concerned. Of course, there is often a link between each half of the game.

- Stop wasting time over the problems. Take control of your own emotions and help the players improve for their second half with well thought out strategies and support. These could include technical, tactical, physical or psychological detail, or a good, old-fashioned 'hearts and minds' chat. Tell them you believe in them and that they are capable of better. It's your choice.

CHAPTER 21

Leadership in Sport

"A person who feels appreciated will always do more than what is expected." – Amy Rees Anderson

My brother once said to me:

"To be a good leader, you have to be able to take your people on a journey."

In the workplace, I believe people work in two ways:

- Through love
- Through fear

What are your thoughts on leadership?

- What is it to you?
- What does it look like in your eyes?
- How does it feel to you and others when you are being led or when you're leading yourself?
- What does it look like and feel like to lead a group of people?

I know a little, having led people in schools and football clubs for many years. At one school I worked at, there were 200 teachers and staff and 2,600 pupils. Trust me, that is a lot of personalities to manage. In the past, I have directly line-managed 18 people at a time. Of these 18, approximately six were exceptional practitioners, six were average and six were inadequate. I would say those ratios are probably the norm in teaching. The best six I didn't need to lead, as they led themselves with classy behaviours; the middle six needed regular monitoring, but once monitored were effective at their jobs; the bottom six were hard work to manage and required rigorous monitoring, support, life coaching and counselling – and they still could not perform consistently. It was a drain on my time and resources, but it was still my duty to support these people. I regard effective leadership as:

> *"The genuine and authentic ability to influence people."*

Now, there are many variables and styles when it comes to leadership. Situations and context are key ingredients, of course, but you have to consider the following:

- How to lead in a certain way.
- Why to lead in a certain way.
- When to lead in a certain way.
- Who to lead in a certain way.
- What to lead in a certain way.

Have you really thought about what qualities a good leader displays? Does leadership in sport differ from leadership in business or education? What is more important in a leader: autocracy or democracy? Or is it a mix of both?

I will attempt to give you my version of effective leadership and what I believe it should look like. In my lifetime, I have worked under more bad leaders than good ones. The nine headteachers I've worked for over the years were varied in ability. One was truly exceptional; three were average and the rest were useless. The useless, overpaid group comprised a variation of blaggers, those with poor people skills, the work shy (yes, you heard it) and bullshitters. They often lacked authenticity, had poor subject knowledge, had no vision and displayed many other traits that are generally negative. But the main areas that were missing from these weak leaders were vision, strategy and an ability to take people on a journey with them. These types of leaders would obviously say unconsciously in their dialect:

- "Me" instead of "we".
- "My" and "I" instead of "our and us".

These small examples are yet again a strong sign that a leader is internally focused. Leaders need many qualities, of course; they need to be approachable, humble, positive, emotionally consistent and generous. They also need to display high levels of integrity. But in very simple terms, I believe leaders need three main qualities:

- A clear vision and strategy that they follow through.
- High levels of subject knowledge in their relevant field.
- People skills.

Why do I say this?

We have all worked for a boss who knows everything about everything and possesses unbelievable knowledge about their subject and chosen career. They might be rubbish with their own emotions and cut you down with harsh words while adopting a draconian and autocratic manner, but because they are so knowledgeable you cannot help but at least respect them, even if they are naturally unlikeable. Then there are the charisma-style bosses who are super savvy at employing a good team around them and often lead with delegation and a democratic approach. They lead with aspiration and praise; they may have little subject knowledge, but they get away with this flaw by keeping their staff motivated. This, in turn, keeps business flowing with charm, as staff members feel consistently valued. However, over the long-term, people can often get annoyed with these types of bosses for not always getting stuff done, as their laissez-faire style means they lack a dynamic and effective approach.

Now, clearly I have been very basic in my evaluation of leadership, but to put it simply, combining these two examples is the key to creating an A-grade leader. When hinged together, these two examples would create an explicitly strong leader with a diverse and relevant subject knowledge that additionally enables staff buy-in with charm, charisma and, mostly importantly, direction. Now, regarding charisma, I am not talking about a David Brent-type 'charm'. (Remember the annoying character from the TV show *The Office?*) I mean sincere, authentic and emotionally intelligent leadership that, when needed, engages hearts and minds. These leaders possess positive traits, such as being in control under pressure, kindness, a caring nature and being both inspirational and aspirational, plus many other facets of what great leaders implement with regularity. These managers are also good decision makers and are not afraid to upset people on occasion.

> *A major rule in leadership is that you cannot keep all people happy all of the time, and that is something the people being led also need to understand better.*

Sometimes people need to be good at following rather than always challenging the system. Football is no different.

Looking at the assessment of leadership and managers in the football industry, Jurgen Klopp stands out for me. I would play for him more than any of his contemporaries. In my opinion, his interesting background, his journey and his unbelievably high levels of emotional intelligence shine through in the media, compared to other managers such as Wenger and Mourinho. Let me emphasise that a manager's media persona isn't necessarily their training ground one, but taking this chapter on face value is important. Forget about results and success for a moment, because we could argue about successful leaders in sport and football for years to come. In sport, I firmly believe it is dangerous to always see success as the ability to win trophies – it is obvious by observing Klopp's professional and personal agenda that he is much greater than that. I truly believe he wants to help the city of Liverpool reconnect and achieve together. He wants to build a club, and he wants to do it with honesty, dignity and pride. In interviews, he regularly smiles and portrays the soft skills that many of his peers do not. He talks openly to the media and regularly uses humour and humility. On the other hand, over the last few years in particular, Wenger has often been defensive and neutral in personality. And, when questioned, 90 per cent of the time he will claim he did not see incidents. Even the average football fan can see straight through these responses.

I believe Mourinho is also a closed, defensive character. When he first came to the premiership he was a breath of fresh air by claiming, with his unbelievable arrogance, that he was the 'special one'. But he is well known to only be around clubs for a short period. Yes, he has been highly successful, but we could get into a debate over whether he's about to be 'found out' concerning his leadership style. And remember that to be an effective leader, you have to manage two ways … up towards the board and down towards your team and staff. You have the board above you putting demands on you to succeed, while the players and staff require your help and guidance. It's a seriously tough job.

I've been able to witness first-hand how good Neil Harris is at Millwall. Around the training ground, he was like a bubble of positivity and whenever I had lunch with him around those round tables at the Calmont Road training ground, or whenever I took part in staff five-a-side games, I always saw him making an effort with the staff, top to bottom. He was just a normal bloke basically, and one of us.

In interviews after defeats, Mourinho regularly blames anyone and everyone but himself – and normally the referee is the one he points the finger at. That is fine for him to say, of course, and occasionally it's natural, and it could be a clever ploy and a conscious choice by him to deflect blame, which can be appropriate for the media. But personally, after 10 years, I have gotten bored of him never admitting he is at fault. His persona changes quickly when he is winning games and getting his way. You could say that's natural. I say it's spoilt and immature. The football chant, "You only sing when you're winning" couldn't be more appropriate for someone like Mourinho. I was brought up from my Crown Woods school days with the following PE department saying ringing through my ears, *"Win in honour and lose in honour."*

I wish we could see more of it at the top level. Dignity is a lost art in the modern game. I acknowledge that Jose is more knowledgeable about football than I will ever be, I just wish, like every football fan, that he would respect the game a little more, however on a serious note, it's a really tough job, which the armchair fan doesn't always appreciate.

What's interesting in the modern premier league arena is that there are now six world-class leaders who have all been highly successful in the past. Klopp, Mourinho, Pochettino, Sarri, Emery and Guardiola. But who is the best? Amazingly, if they fail to win the league, five of them will probably be perceived as failures by their own supporters! This is complete nonsense. I feel this national epidemic amongst supporters, who lack knowledge and have unrealistic mindsets, is incredibly unfair, and another reason why linking leadership success with winning trophies is not valid. To this day, the Gary Rowett sacking by Birmingham City still baffles me. Wow, poor bloke!

Here are a couple of questions for you to consider:

- Is leadership all about adding value?
- Which leaders ensure their teams make the most progress with the resources available?

Surely Sean Dyche, Eddie Howe and Chris Hughton are in the top group of managers. They have been doing the business for years. In rugby, Eddie Jones and Clive Woodward are legends of sport, as is the one and only John Wooden in basketball. Many years ago, Wooden was quoted as saying, "I think that in any group activity – whether it be business, sports or family – there has to be leadership or it won't be successful."

> The educationalist William Arthur Wood once stated that:
> "Leadership is based on inspiration, not domination, on cooperation, not intimidation."

So, what about the leaders who rule through fear? The ones who have one setting, which is to intimidate people; the ones who regularly belittle and supress the thoughts and feelings of others. I regard them as narcissistic leaders who are often passive aggressive in approach and act friendly one day and cold the next. They generally want control over people. They struggle to delegate and when they do, complain about your work. Often they hide behind emails and are emotionally all over the place. You must not hate these leaders, however, but instead feel sorry for them. They are more than likely afraid and living life with fear instead of hope. They are naturally negative instead of positive, and although they won't show they are scared, they are certainly feeling it inside. Whenever they grind you down with these behaviours, just remember that better is around the corner and that they are intrinsically lonely people and will have few authentic relationships in the workplace and beyond.

CHAPTER 22

Football Philosophy: The Prizes and the Pitfalls

Tiki-taka is a load of s**t – passing for the sake of passing. I won't allow my brilliant players to fall for all that rubbish." – Pep Guardiola

Spain's Tiki-taka, Holland's Total Football and Jurgen Klopp's Heavy Metal Football ... the list goes on. What is your football philosophy? Do you have one? Where did it derive from? If you had the best 11 players in the league, how would you like your team to play? In contrast, if you had the 11 worst players at your disposal, what would be your philosophical approach?

I'll be honest with you about my philosophy. I want to be involved in winning teams, and I don't understand managers who say, "I cannot have my team play in that style as it is against my philosophy." Fair enough, it is your life and your decision. But surely getting three points week in, week out holds no better feeling and it is what first-team football is all about. I laugh at managers who change their philosophy after a few losses or play out from the back in their first seven pre-season games, but when the real season kick offs are so panic stricken in the first five minutes that they scream aimlessly at their keeper and defenders to stop taking risks by playing out, and tell them to smash it up on the pitch for the next 46 games. It's hilarious and it happens all the time. Why? Because the 'philosophy' which the manager created, promoted and bored the players to death with simply got thrown in the bin due to a lack of emotional control, confidence and fear from, yes, you guessed it, the leader.

In my opinion, this is where the amateur or weaker managers often get football philosophy wrong. Why? Because at first-team level the game is about winning, and if you can't get the exact players you want through the door, because your budget does not allow it, you have to adapt your philosophy, plain and simple. But managers, in non-league especially, get this aspect wrong, unless they are really lucky and have the budget to get the players that suit their philosophy.

Let me explain myself further. I teach and coach in a way that reflects my wish to witness good football. I categorically do not want to be involved in a team that plays crappy long ball for 90 minutes of every game. I refuse to label myself as having that philosophy with the players because it is painful, no fun and boring to be involved in. I would like to emphasise that I want to coach a team that utilises its strengths to the best of its abilities; a team that controls the controllables; a team that maximises its strengths around a philosophy of creativity and clever, intelligent tactics via set plays, and more. This is where training to be a PE teacher helped me. On the old national curriculum was a teaching and learning strand called 'outwitting opponents'. The single and only aim of pupils nationally was to learn how to be cleverer than their opponents. So, therefore, pupils of all ages had to learn tactical philosophy. If our opposition pressed poorly against us in basketball, football or hockey, we were very quick to assess the situation. As an example, in basketball, imagine that the opposition had chosen to press us high up the court.

The questions to the students would then be:

- Are they pressing effectively?
- Is there a less athletic player in the team we can isolate to get out of this full court press?
- Where is all the space to hurt the opposition now they are pressing us?

My point?

- ✓ The philosophy has flexibility.
- ✓ The philosophy is not fixed.
- ✓ The philosophy has a context.

CHAPTER 22 - FOOTBALL PHILOSOPHY: THE PRIZES AND THE PITFALLS

✓ The philosophy, therefore, might have to change.

So, let me pose this question to you: Why do managers have a philosophy that plays out from the back time and again when the opponents press you, the players cannot do it consistently and the team is always mid table? Let me explain further. If you haven't got the time in your training schedule to make these players better, then you are failing to work out that your philosophy is flawed. My point is that the meaning of the word *manager* is by name and by nature. You have to *manage the situation in front of you!* Smell it, sense it, feel it and observe it.

Your job is to manage the situation, as follows:

- Find a system that suits the players you have in front of you, and not the other way round. End of story.
- Educate your players about how, when, why and where to adopt your philosophy and simply outwit your opponents, week after week. That's the essence of sport, you see. You use the tools available to suit the needs of the job in hand.

Remember that Pep Guardiola handpicks his players to play to his philosophy, but he works at one of the richest clubs in the world. Another baffling example is when managers sign players and then ask them to do things they are not capable of, or that do not fit with the philosophy. I would like to emphasise that the methodology previously mentioned is for first-team level, where results are everything. At youth and academy level, the philosophy simply has to change to meet the needs of the bigger process, which is, of course, to develop the complete player. At youth level, results are truly irrelevant and to all those coaches out there who think it's the World Cup week in, week out, let me tell you … chill out!

Your only job as a youth coach is to make the players in your team better players and better people – that's it.

It's easy. Remember that results can often mask development, as a coach's ego can take over with the, 'Look at me, I am great' mentality. So ensure you are implementing improvements in your players week after week, which should be the only parameter of success. However, I will end this chapter with the nugget that learning to win games is also a part of the development process, but, in my opinion, this should not override your duty around player progress. It is the 'prove or improve' debate all over again, and it's for you to decide, not me.

CHAPTER 23

Follow the Process ... and you get Progress

"That's the plan at the minute. The season-long plan was a tour, on to the Olympics and on after that to the Vuelta. That's still the outline at the minute, as we go through the next phase and with the peak at the Olympics, but we will assess it as we go along. All being well, that's what we will be doing." – Dave Brailsford.

There is nothing more frustrating than hearing football managers stating, "This is a must-win game today," or, "We have to get the three points."

After all, that's bloody obvious! What is actually going to happen after these nonsense statements? Imagine this ... a 'three-point fairy' turns up every match day and displays a magic wand for your team to gain victory. Or, alternatively, I see the reality more like this: All the minor variables of an effective team performance come together, including what you do in possession, without possession, in transition, hydration, mindset, passion, togetherness, and the list goes on. But overall, a well thought out game plan, individually and collectively, to get a desired result.

After all, I call football 'movement chess'. It is like any other invasion game out there, including basketball, rugby, hockey and netball. The priority is to outthink your opponents. Ebere Eze, the QPR starlet, laughed at me when I said this phrase to him once in a player meeting. Six months later, he apologised after eventually understanding the meaning. Ebere, the player on the front cover, will feature again later in the book.

But this is my point: For success to happen in elite sport, you cannot think about the end point (victory) too often or too early on a match day. You need to stay in the now. Other sporting examples of the process include:

- How to achieve a gold medal at the Olympics.
- A strategy for a five-day test match in cricket.
- Winning the gruelling Tour de France.

All these examples are about having a plan and strategy in their own right. And, as the title of this chapter suggests … a process! The 'off-the-cuff' football of the past is long gone, which is why the dinosaurs of the game are being found out.

I have been lucky and flattered to be called a strategist. I take great pride in always trying to think ahead and see the long game in every sporting decision I make, either by myself or with colleagues. Short-termism is a great saying and it is rife in football, business and life. Although occasionally we have to adopt this strategy, most of the time coaches and educators must try and work against it.

Examples of this are:

- Using players who are unfit in order to get the win in the next match, but risking them suffering a long-term injury.
- Playing with certain crappy spoiling tactics that get the team through sticky patches of average form.
- Trying to stitch someone up in business for a quick monetary gain, but hindering a long-term relationship due to selfishness and stupidity.

All of these examples will eventually cause the decision maker to fail over the long term. They always do. So think about the game of football and why so many managers fail mainly because of their use of an ineffective strategy and process. As previously mentioned, one of my annoyances is managers who neglect to deploy a proper game plan and constantly chat about the three points. The three points and victories just won't happen if the team doesn't play well consistently via the platform given to them by their manager. So think about the next set of questions.

CHAPTER 23 - FOLLOW THE PROCESS ... AND YOU GET PROGRESS

How do you get a team to play well consistently?

- Answer: With a process (and good players help, of course).

What is a process?

- Answer:
  - A game plan and strategy, as individuals, positional pairings and units all have a job description (i.e. defence, midfield and attack).
  - Being told by your manager what you need to do as an individual and how you can use your personal attributes to contribute to the team ethos and identity, which incorporates what you personally do both with and without the ball.
  - Knowing how the team operates as a whole, and how the team strategy operates with and without the ball. Basically, knowing what to do when the team defends as an 11, and then attacks as an 11. Again, I reiterate, this is a plan ... a process.

The above seems quite simple, doesn't it? Follow the process and results just come. Ha ha, it's not as simple as that, as we all know. Bobby Robson, the legendary ex-England manager, said the following to the press after a defeat whilst he was boss at Newcastle United:

> *"Gents, sometimes I don't think you realise something about this game. I may have employed the best tactics in the world, but have you lot not realised that I have an opposition of 11 men, five subs, a manager and his assistant trying to prevent me from implementing my game plan and wanting to win themselves. It's not that easy."*

Superb language and understanding from a great man! So yes, winning in sport is not that easy. If managers have a win rate of around 50 to 60 per cent, they are flying in their career and most likely keeping their job. It is only the greatest ever managers that are above the 70 per cent bracket.

However, putting the Bobby Robson quote aside, think about this:

Have you ever wondered why many potentially great coaches with the best plans still fail?

> Answer: Because their emotional control is zero.

The language they give to players is so emotion led that they lose sight of the actual process. Many leaders don't have a plan in the first place, and they often can only say, "Be more aggressive" or, "Run around more." And limited communication equates to a limited chance of a successful result! Even so, having a process doesn't guarantee anything either, but what it does do is give teams and athletes a greater chance of success. Gareth Southgate was class personified when England conceded late against Columbia in the 2018 World Cup. The camera scanned to him and you could see him say to his team, "Stay calm." His body language oozed class.

Throughout my managing career, fans have always asked me on a match day prior to kick-off, "Steve, are we going to win today?"

My response is the same every time. "Not a clue, mate. All I can control is preparing the team, giving them a game plan to follow and seeing where we go with it. Who knows if we will win? I haven't got a crystal ball. Hopefully, our process and strategy will get us a result."

So, in summary, if you manage or coach a team:

- DO NOT let your emotions decide key strategic decisions for your team. It will mostly do you and them harm. The occasional rant is OK, it's natural and it can sometimes be effective. But normally what's required is a good, old-fashioned hearts and minds message.

- You need an A, B, C and D plan, but if you get to Z you're in trouble!

- Have a process, not only for on the pitch and the players, but one in your own head about how to control what Dr Steve Peters calls the 'chimp' as explained in his book, *The Chimp Paradox*. Otherwise, the three points is rarely happening and accelerated progress for your team will never be made. When I was a teacher, I taught the craziest classes who ignored everything I said to them. My one self-talk strategy was to stay calm. If I lost my rag it was game over. Any teacher will tell you: often you need an emotional game plan as well as a practical and a physical one.

I have always said, "If you cannot speak and act well, you cannot teach or coach well."

The best coaches are the most articulate ones. So look at developing your speech, body language and vocabulary in order to help improve your message.

SECTION FOUR
Second Half – Teamwork Training

This section of six chapters focuses on the importance of resilience for athlete development, behavioural psychology and sport psychology concepts. It also looks into the importance of group dynamics in terms of cohesion, cooperation, human compatibility and communication in an elite environment context.

CHAPTER 24

The Importance of TEAMwork!

The Team Behind the TEAM, and the Importance of Emotional Connection

"I didn't want to be the coach who wins, but the coach who educates." – Vincent del Bosque

During my lifetime, I have worked in many different professional environments, and I'm fortunate because this diversity has made me who I am today. Much of my work wasn't as glamorous as the professional football industry, but these differing experiences have enabled me to influence it. Many times it's been proven that different professional and life experiences can bring new ideas to the table in the modern workplace. These are often more abstract and creative. I've had many colleagues whom I've regarded as the kindest, most passionate and most loyal people anyone could wish for and, over the years, I have felt enthused about supporting them daily to ensure our place of work is the most aspirational and supportive place on earth. I would be distraught if I discovered a former colleague didn't label me as a team player. In the professional football environment, players also need to feel valued, as they do in any job. But what about the topic I regard as the most important factor in order to achieve excellence? The staff, of course! It used to really wind me up when headteachers were overly focused on how the kids were. Let me explain. They often had 150 staff members who loved working in schools, so my theory is, "If you keep the staff happy, the kids are going to get a good deal anyway."

Many have said this cheesy quote, but it really does work: "Teamwork makes the dream work."

What CEOs, headteachers, business leaders and football club chairmen need to understand is that helping the staff achieve is the number one priority. In my view, if the staff members are unhappy, any business or sports team is destined for failure over the long term. So, what makes happy staff? Is it their pay packet or having self-worth and feeling valued? Research and opinion tells us, without doubt, that it's the latter. Often in football, and sport in general, enthusiasts and fanatics have their favourite players and athletes. For whatever reason, whether they are a goalkeeper, defender, midfielder, attacker or bowler, the fan will identify a trait in them that they love. Most kids love the flair players, such as Messi, Ronaldo and Bale in football, and Tendulkar in cricket, to name a few. These sportsmen are all winners, of course, but what about all the other, more low-key players who help them (and therefore the team) achieve greater glory? These so-called lesser players perform selflessly every game, week after week, in order for the so-called star players to be able to express themselves. These players help win games for the greater good of the team, but are often under the radar. In my experience, only those with a trained eye can spot these players.

For example:

- Kante of Chelsea is renowned for being the best ball winner in existence.
- Deschamps, from the great French team that took home the World Cup in 1998, was known as the 'water carrier' for his effort and energy.
- Martin Johnson, England's rugby captain of World Cup-winning fame from 2003, who was the complete opposite in playing style compared to Jonny Wilkinson's flair and physique, was the physical enforcer.

So, in terms of staff, have you ever thought about the other workers who metaphorically stand behind the first-team manager or head coach and help them lead and inspire the team?

CHAPTER 24 - THE IMPORTANCE OF TEAMWORK!

Elite and highly functioning clubs, teams and institutions do not become elite by fluke. Google, the highly acclaimed internet search engine, is famous for providing a superb working culture for their staff. Their CEO, Sundar Pichai, stated, "Being able to create a well-balanced team with a positive culture is more important than the individual employees who comprise the team. When we talk about performance review, we talk about individuals, not teams. How the team operates and the culture of the team is way more important than who is on the team because as humans, we like to pigeonhole everybody. We like to categorise everyone. The key thing that's missing over here is context."

Football clubs are often no different. The average football fan pays their hard-earned money to see their team go out and perform on a Saturday. As far as most of these fans are aware, the manager simply picks the team and tells them to win. But the trained eye knows that it is more complex than that and involves the variables of skill, team organisation, physicality, fitness, player mentality, group cohesion and maybe a little bit of luck. These are the things that get a result at the end of the game.

Over the years, the poor off-the-field relationship between Manchester United's Andy Cole and Teddy Sheringham, and how they managed to put this friction aside on match day, has often been highlighted. England cricketer Kevin Pieterson also allegedly caused rifts with many teammates, but he managed to put those aside to produce results at the highest level for his country. It's certainly not rare for athletes to clash in the elite sport environment, but these examples ended in positive outcomes and results for the team, and they say much about everyone concerned, both professionally and emotionally. It quantifies what I believe the meaning of professional really is – so well done fellas.

We often talk about the meaning of professional, but this mainly concerns the players who are out on the pitch and performing. But what about the professionalism, cohesion and group dynamics of the 'team behind the team'? I think the importance of this term is undervalued by many outsiders. So, have you ever thought how the success or failure of a team could be down to the team behind the team?

I rarely lose it these days, but I once did with a youth player at Millwall. Back in my early teaching days, it was hard not to regularly lose your temper. The behaviour of the kids was often unsafe and fights happened hourly … literally. The Millwall player in question basically did not conform to what I felt was the blueprint of our exceptional academy culture and vision. He was simply asked as a favour by another team member to pick up some house keys from the third floor of a building. The player in question refused and responded with, "Why should I? I can't be arsed." I was fuming over his laziness and response, but generally with age and experience, I have evolved into a calmer and more holistic version of myself, and in most situations I am now the voice of reason.

This scenario may seem like nothing to you, and you may think it has no correlation to on-pitch performances. If this is the case, that's fine. You have your own opinions and experiences and it's your choice to feel that way as an educator. You may well understand the behaviour of the player who could not be bothered to help a teammate with an off-the-field issue. Evidently, I did not agree with this player's behaviour and never will, and at the time I told him how hugely disappointed I was. I also condemned his lazy actions. Far too often in British society, we look at the calibre of people, when in fact we simply need to look at the character of people! Schools are the worst for this. Lives are defined by academic results. Wouldn't it be great if they were defined by character? Food for thought!

My argument is that we talk about many aspects at the top level regarding what it takes to be elite, but in any business, selflessness is a huge part of an effective performance culture. And yes, sport is a business! It is an easy word to say, but in my opinion it's not so easy to implement, especially in the selfish society we inhabit today. As an example, social media influences this 'look at me behaviour', which in turn promotes selfishness and selfies on Instagram. My advice was simple at the time, and it still is to this day. It's important to adopt an approach and a mindset of 'we, not me'. Put simply, this means thinking about others before yourself.

On the flip side, if you had 11 starting players in football, or any team sport for that matter, who were all selfish people, what do you think the likelihood would be of that team being a success? Elite sport can be rife with selfishness and in my experience, I'd say a team like this may fluke a win or two in the short-term, but over a season or career, long-term success is highly unlikely. However, please feel free to disagree. I welcome it. In support of this story, this country needs to get a grip in general in how it rewards and sanctions people.

Why am I telling you this story of selfishness, and what is its relevance to the team behind the team?

I'm sure you have heard terminology like 'marginal gains' in business and performance genres, and how the 'one percenters' create success. Mark Warburton, the former Nottingham Forest and Glasgow Rangers manager says the term 'adding value' regularly in TV interviews. As mentioned earlier, I have worked with some so-called professionals who would not even care that one player had refused to help out his teammate by fetching the house key. Many of you reading this might feel the same and perceive it as making a fuss over nothing. Many coaches may assume that because this issue is not about passing, shooting or performing poorly on the grass, it doesn't matter and therefore has nothing to do with match-day results. I will say, sadly for those of you who act and think in this way, you are very wrong.

For me, the details around team dynamics are massive. Culture is everything. I would argue that this was as big as anything else I had to deal with in my working week while I was at Millwall. It had to be, and yes, I may be perceived as mad, but I do not care or regret it. My former headteacher, Paul Petty, used to say to me, "Steve, if you watch the pennies, the pounds will take care of themselves." This is a great quote, which I have always adhered too. So, therefore, the issue about a player's house keys is a not a one per cent issue. It a 10 per cent issue as far as I am concerned, hence my passion for these marginal gains. Let me explain why. How poor is it that we as coaches, teachers and educators talk about the importance of kindness, empathy, selflessness, resilience, grit and the one per cent gains in relation to group cohesion and performance on a match day, if we do not act on it ourselves during the week leading up to the game?

My advice is:

1. Do it and show it *consistently* in yourself and your own behaviour.
2. Understand that this process is *not* merely confined to the pitch.
3. Think about the *long-term effects of one small moment* and its potential damaging outcomes for team culture and, therefore, success on the pitch.

Players are asked all the time to support each other on the pitch and are often told by managers to run that "extra 10 yards" for each other. That day, I visibly saw the player on the wrong end of this altercation get angry, upset and annoyed by his lazy teammate. When I asked him afterwards he told me that he felt betrayed. The irony of this story is that the player who was refused help getting his keys was the same player who he gave a lift into work every day. Yes, you heard it … you could not make this up. Simply, this type of selfish behaviour is not acceptable if a club or sporting team wants sustained success. Let us forget football here and talk human to human and man to man (or man to woman, and so on). One elite player has basically stuck two fingers up to a teammate and said, albeit passively, "I don't respect you, pal." Now, what could or would happen if I ignored this issue as the person in charge? Could the players:

> Grow further apart emotionally?

> Begin to dislike each other?

It's pretty unlikely these two players would perform well together in a team and gain success with this lack of off-the-field unity. The paying fans want passion, and passion is created by team bonds. If the argument between the players was ignored, sustained success was never going to happen – and all over a simple set of bloody house keys. The reason that 'behaviour for learning' policies exist in schools is simple. Once the behaviour of people improves, so does learning and culture. In summary:

- Do you work harder for teammates and colleagues that you like and care about?

CHAPTER 24 - THE IMPORTANCE OF TEAMWORK!

- Has productivity improved because of these closer relationships?
- Will a team perform better if the team behind the team works together with kindness, selflessness, passion and cohesion?
- Are you judging players on calibre instead of character?
- Finally, a team will perform better and with greater precision if marginal gains are addressed when they arise and everyone in the building understands their importance. Player-driven standards are the only way. Ignore them at your peril.

As the ex-Spanish manager, Vicente del Bosque, once said, "Each coach has his own personality. My leadership is based on human values, on sharing and on being friendly. If you only know about football you are lost."

CHAPTER 25

No Dickheads! The Importance of Group Dynamics for Success in TEAMS

"No one, not rock stars, not professional athletes, not software billionaires, and not even geniuses, ever makes it alone."
– Malcom Gladwell

Malcom Gladwell has been mentioned in this book already, but the famous author of several books deserves another shout out for this genius quote.

As mentioned in the previous chapter, how many times have you thought deeply about the teams or groups of people you have played or worked with? What about the annoying and disruptive people that have caused mayhem, whether consciously or unconsciously?

Now, I admit it, I've stolen the 'no dickheads policy' from the mighty All Blacks rugby team, who are well known for adopting this practice and strategy to ensure players and staff don't cause any disruption. In actual fact, the All Blacks stole this from the Sydney Swans, who are an Australian Rules football team, which is yet another example of the importance of sharing good practice across the globe.

It would be mindless to think that group cohesion at the elite level of any sport is only improved by a few team mates. I truly believe elite athletes and the team they are involved in not only show high standards of performance on the field, but also their off-the-field behaviours are elite. High performance teams are not created by fluke. Simply everyone contributes. And if they don't, my point is:

- Why is this not the case?

- Do some people think it is not their duty or role to improve team morale and culture?
- For those of us who are involved in a team, whether for sport or work, surely everyone wants to be involved in a high performing one?
- Are some people so narcissistic they enjoy being part of things that fail?
- Isn't one of the purposes of life to help others be successful and not to hinder them?

After all, socialisation is a big part of the human experience. The achievers in life get up every day to improve, and that is a massive quality. Some people have got it and some haven't. What are you: a lazy floater or a go-getter?

Most people have to work for 50 years of their lives. Maybe some of you have been lucky enough to play elite team sports for 20 years or so. Whatever your journey, these differing experiences contribute to your own self-worth, as well as improving others'. These personal processes are the key to a successful team and, therefore, a more fulfilling life. If the aspiration of team leaders and businesses was to only appoint good people before good players and workers, then surely teams across the globe would have a greater chance of performing better. Do you agree?

> *Using football as an example, if managers think that a good player doesn't have to be a good person they are wrong. I regard these types of managers as lacking an ethical and moral compass, because what gives footballers the right to be a dickhead?*

The question above is posed to you because some coaches and managers sadly accept that it is OK to be disruptive if the person in question happens to kick a ball around well. Well, I don't think so, and you shouldn't either. Sean Dyche wouldn't sign a dickhead and neither would Eddie Howe.

CHAPTER 25 - NO DICKHEADS! THE IMPORTANCE OF GROUP DYNAMICS FOR SUCCESS IN TEAMS

Now, before you disagree abruptly and challenge my thoughts about this theory by saying that it is only the results that matter, I would like to add that I can understand your point of view to a small extent, but in the long-term, group dynamics will never improve when there are dickheads in the building. And if group dynamics are poor, then the team, regardless of what level they are working or playing at, is destined to underperform in the medium and long-term.

So, in the first instance, the self-awareness required to not be a disruptive influence is important. As previously mentioned in this book, most of you are probably aware of the David Brent character from the television show *The Office*. His behaviour showed that he was lacking self-awareness in a big way.

Below, I have highlighted the common personality traits of dickheads:

- **The constant jokers**: They are ones who pick the wrong moments to indulge in banter. Basically, they are the types who laugh at their own jokes. They can often be effective in groups, but lack the social and emotional intelligence to build truly unique relationships. Thus group dynamics and personal relationships are negatively affected.

- **The blockers:** These people make life difficult for everyone by being 100 per cent problem focused. They always do things by the book or are masters at constantly creating problems to people's solutions by saying, "I am not sure we can do that…"

- **The naturally negative people:** I call them the 'Happy Hoovers.' These people are elite at sucking up happiness from others. They see the glass as half-empty and lack the resilience or self-awareness to understand how they drag people down with every comment and every word they say. These people are not who you would want in the trenches with you if life got tough. In a sporting context, these types of teammates or work colleagues often use blame as their only way out. They have a 'can't do' mentality. As an ex-colleague of mine used to say when he met these people, "Bore off, mate."

- **The social loafers:** These people tend to sit back and watch the ship sinking, while washing their hands of any blame. The bigger the group size, the more they disappear into the background. It's a bit like the TV show *The Apprentice* I suppose, where in the first show of each series, Sir Alan normally saves the losing captain for having the balls to head the team up in the first place. Now, Alan Sugar is people savvy and often despises the silent assassins who sit back and allow failure to happen. He doesn't accept a flaky approach to group dynamics. This is known in psychology terms as the Ringelmann effect. I call these people 'passive dickheads'. They are often quietly harmful and will finger point behind other people's backs.

- **The "I'm never wrong" dickheads:** These people never say sorry or admit to any wrongdoing, and they therefore find it hard to build truly great relationships. These are the types of performers or colleagues who blag it when they are in the wrong. They normally deceive people when they perform at an average level, and boast when they actually exceed expectations, but they will never admit the opposite. They say words like "I" and not "we". I call them 'eye specialists', as they're people who say, "I did this and I did that."

So, whether you are reading this as a player, coach, leader or merely as a member of a group, please promote and contribute to a no dickhead policy in your workplace or team!

> As the All Blacks are famous for saying,
> "Better people make better All Blacks."

But forget about the All Blacks here. *Better* people make a *better* life.

CHAPTER 26

Sports Teams: IMPROVE them or REPLACE them?

The power of 'Learning conversations'

"In the supermarket, you have eggs. Class one, class two, class three. Some are more expensive than others and some give you better omelettes. So, when the class one eggs are in Waitrose and you cannot go there, you have a problem." – Jose Mourinho

A premier league player who is a client recently texted me and said thank you for all my help in getting him back to better levels of performance. What did I really do, however? It goes as simply as this:

- He contacted me.
- We had a conversation.
- I asked how he felt and why he felt it.
- I gave him some possible solutions.
- He felt better about himself and his life, and thus played better football.

My stance was primarily a questions-based approach, or, for more business-minded people, I used coaching to help this athlete with his thought processes, so he had the opportunity to solve his problems for himself. I often have the answers to development but choose not to give them to clients, as I believe, with my help, they can find the solutions themselves. Most importantly, however, I tell them to go and talk to their sports coach to agree on a set of interventions to help support them with their blip in form. It still shocks me how many elite players are scared to talk to their coach about vulnerable issues.

So, let me give you a scenario:

A player you manage has been having a bad run of form over several games. A week ago, year ago or a month ago, they were 9/10 every week and everyone was singing their praises and saying how good they were. *What do you do?*

If you apply this experience to any business or education, it's clear that any individual, sports team or business has good and bad days. Therefore, questions around these scenarios could be:

- Do these people/athletes turn into bad players or work colleagues overnight?
- Does a period of poor performance amount to a bad player/colleague?
- Have you ever made the link between bad form and a bad coach or manager?

I'll let you reflect on these...

People are so varied and complex, and it still amazes me when managers across all industries have a fixed mindset towards what they want, rather than the needs of the individual they lead or the company they work for. After all, in managerial sporting terms, that's the art of player and team progression: differentiating to meet the learning needs of all players all of the time. Basically, what I'm saying is that every manager's job is quite simple and straightforward, isn't it? Surely it is to maximise the skills of every individual and get this to fit into the team dynamic and journey. The hard part is telling people you have tried to help that they are still not performing.

As I mentioned before, many people probably haven't heard the term 'assessment for learning'. To put it simply, this is probably the most significant key driver in institutional improvement in schools, along with lots of great teachers, of course. Whenever I started work at a failing school, AFL was what the whole improvement process was built around. So, what is it? Let me explain. It's how various assessment methods improve the performance of the people in the building. These include:

> - **Self-assessment** – Knowledge of one's own strengths and weaknesses.
> - **Manager/coach assessment** – Coach's knowledge of players' strengths and weaknesses.
> - **Peer assessment** – Peers/teammates' knowledge of your strengths and weaknesses.
> - **Summative assessment** - Using data, test scores, testing and numbers to assess players and performance.
> - **Formative assessment** – Using learning conversations, target setting and scaffolded learning techniques to discuss with athletes what they do well and how to fine-tune strategies to improve.

What I am trying to explain is that formative assessment strategies (to inform the athlete of things they need to do to improve) are the number one facet for athlete development, if the desired outcome is effective accelerated learning. Some of the people I have worked with have heard me call this method 'learning conversations'. Managers in most jobs and industries often have the subject knowledge, but their intervention techniques (or lack of) are the reason why those in their charge have extended periods of bad form. I recently spoke to one premier league player who is on loan to a league two club. He said his manager knew loads about tactics, but ignored all his players' phone calls, which meant that no one could talk to him about any issues they had. Surely that cannot help performance! Of course, we know that poor performance is inevitable at any level in sport. So, the question that needs to be asked is this:

> *Why don't more coaches act to improve the players they serve instead of always replacing them?*

My experiences of academy football at professional club level as a player, and during my time in non-league football, were appalling. I had two, maybe three managers that actually had the subject knowledge to help me perform better. One of them didn't teach me a thing in the whole time I was there. But let's move on to the good ones. Back home in Sussex, Glen Geard taught me nuggets of technical knowledge that I'd never previously heard of and made me feel like a million dollars on the pitch. Richard Thomas, another coach I played under, formerly the assistant manager at Notts County, was a super organised manager and he always made us play with a plan. And I seem to remember that 25 years ago, Frank (Steve) Phythian, who now works for Sussex FA, was ridiculed for writing notes for his half-time team talk. These days, however, that's the done thing. Fair play to Frank, he was years ahead of his time! I have a funny story from the time when the actor Tamer Hassan was my manager and the chairman at Greenwich Borough Football Club. He came into training one evening with a determined look on his face and shouted that we were on a 'double bubble' for the next three games, but only if we won them all. That soon motivated us, and the film star had to reel out the £50 notes after the third game and third victory. That was a funny night. The other managers I've had, in general, were so poor I have nothing good to say about them. Most of the time, they picked you to play, moaned at you for 90 minutes and a week later replaced you with someone else. They were the ones who were performing poorly, not us. The player 'merry-go-round' is common in non-league due to most players not being contracted. This is why so many highly talented players who get released by professional clubs between the ages of 18 and 21 struggle at semi-professional level. I have always felt that these players need the time to learn a different type of direct football, but are too often discarded. However, that's changed massively in the last five years, as 4G surfaces and better coaches in non-league mean that more teams are now trying to pass it with a more aesthetic looking style of play. It's my opinion that the best passing teams in the leagues I've played in the last 15 years have been Bognor and Dulwich. When Gavin Rose and Junior Kadi get their teams 'popping it', they are as good as pros. It is also no coincidence that they have the surfaces that enable a passing style and football that looks good on the eye.

CHAPTER 26 - SPORTS TEAMS: IMPROVE THEM OR REPLACE THEM?

The football league loan window has been an interesting strategy. This means that managers at this level need to understand that the players in the building are the players that have to stay until the next transfer window. Managers and coaches, therefore, have no choice, as they can't replace the players they have with wholesale changes. This means they have to work with the ones they have at their disposal. Consequently, they have to get creative when making the players better, instead of doing the potentially easy and normal option of getting rid of them and recruiting new players. Now, I am not undermining the pressure that many top-level managers are under. All team managers in every sport carry that burden of pressure to get results. I get it, as it is a results-based business, but my experiences in my career have helped me create a different mindset towards development, which is as follows:

The kids in the building at a school cannot be replaced like sports teams can.

As I stated earlier, in schools you have to work, work and work to make the pupils achieve and improve – you can't just replace them; they're going to be with you for five years. You don't have the same choices as a football club, which can handpick each and every one of the athletes they sign.

So, in summary, player improvement requires:

- Knowledge of the sport or subject you work in.
- AFL strategies that are rigorous and not flaky.
- The ability to impart sound knowledge to your athletes and staff so that they understand in a crystal clear fashion what they do well and what they need to do to be better.

Otherwise, replacing them is the only strategy you have available to you. My point is: Why *wouldn't* you have both?

CHAPTER 27

Behaviour Management or Behaviour for Learning?

If a child does not know how to read – we teach
If a child does not know how to swim – we teach
If a child does not know how to multiply – we teach
If a child does not know how to drive – we teach
If a child does not know how to behave – we punish
- Tom Herner, 1998

I have split this chapter into *operational* and *strategic* behavioural concepts. First of all, behaviour for learning can be identified as follows:

- Positive – the leader emphasises and raises expectations, and is not focused on the negative behaviours of the individual or group.
- It is centred on effective relationships between teams and/or individuals and their teacher/coach.
- It values and rewards behaviour, which helps to maximise and accelerate learning.
- It sets attainable targets for behaviour, based on the unique circumstances of the individual or group.
- It is relevant and applied to all people at all stages and ages.

Operational Behaviour for Learning: Classroom-based Focus

In my final job as an assistant headteacher, I was asked to teach maths to a bottom set, year nine class. This group of fourteen year olds was labelled the worst class in a school of 1,800 pupils. I had never taught maths before and, ironically, had failed my maths GCSE the first time round, so, trust me, I needed a growth mindset for this latest life challenge!

I walked into that classroom for the first time knowing I was in for the biggest challenge of my teaching career to date. I had shit subject knowledge and a nutty class awaited me. What could be worse? Prior to this job, I had been a senior behaviour specialist at two schools and supported local government. So, apparently, I was the 'man that can'. Additionally, over the previous decade, I had helped support the charity London Challenge by mentoring failing and struggling teachers across inner city schools. I was honoured to receive special recognition for a decade's service to London education. Apparently, I was the 'expert' who people turned to when they needed help, support and advice. I was perceived as the good cop amongst staff. A huge motivator for me was to help teachers develop and improve. By this stage in my career, I had supported and mentored hundreds of teaching professionals. Now it was time to practice what I preached!

Most teachers, coaches and educators are familiar with terminology, such as:

- Lesson objectives – This means what learners are supposed to have learnt by the end of the lesson/session.
- Session plans/lesson plans – This refers to the planning and preparation that goes into every lesson/session, which is documented to help the teacher teach and the pupil learn.

Most educators would link the above terms to teaching, learning and hopefully the knowledge pupils will need to have understood and applied by the end of the lesson. Yes, you heard it … knowledge! Ofsted, the government numpties and educational autocrats, state that every pupil has to make progress in every single lesson. However, this class was so badly behaved that progress for them was not about learning maths. It was about not telling each other to "fuck off". I needed a different approach and this was not the approach that would normally take place in a typical learning environment. The textbook was folded several times and thrown out of the window pretty swiftly. This lot couldn't even sit on a chair for five minutes without getting bored and calling each other, or me, a prick. When I took them on, throwing pens across the room was standard behaviour, along with putting Blu Tack in each other's hair. Added to all of this, cussing someone's mother was second nature, along with answering back with swear words to every request I made. So, understandably, this situation was tough and as stressful as I had ever known.

Alternative strategies were therefore required for this very 'different' group of young people. Bear in mind that for 14 years prior to this experience, I had worked at hardcore inner London schools, so I already had vast experiences of low-level disruption, gang culture and a general lack of conformity, but this lot were on another level. Therefore, the need to be creative with my 'lesson objectives' for this class was off the scale. For the first six weeks, I admit I had to go 'maverick' and slightly alternative, so please try not to laugh, be shocked, surprised or upset.

On the classroom whiteboard, instead of writing the learning objectives, as is traditional, I wrote the behaviour objectives. These were as follows:

- Please do not hit anyone today
- Please do not cuss anyone's mother today
- Please do not throw things across the classroom today
- Please do not swear at anyone today
- Please try and be smiley today
- Please leave your happy hoover at home today

On the interactive whiteboard, which sat visibly next to the B4L whiteboard, I wrote out the maths learning objectives. This was what they were actually meant to be learning academically, along with enhancing and improving their behaviour, of course. The lesson objective read:

> *"Learn how to calculate the area of three different shapes, and implement this knowledge into a three mark test question."*

So, let me explain my main reasons for approaching the class with this strategy. Having taught in the toughest and most deprived schools in existence, I've had to learn quickly and adapt my approach to certain classes. One of the main skills I acquired was the need to understand my target audience as quickly as humanly possible. Who could I get on my side? Who were the ringleaders? Additionally, once that was achieved, I then had to ask myself:

> Why would I even bother teaching the maths element of the lesson and see it as my main priority, when the pupils can't even sit in a chair or go without cussing each other's mothers every two minutes?

The same process applies to player culture at a football club. If the players are messing around all the time then this affects learning outcomes and climate, which then affects results. And to put it bluntly, if people cannot behave properly they cannot learn properly. This group of pupils couldn't even sit in their seat for more than two minutes without jumping up and asking to leave the classroom for the toilet. And this was all 17 of them asking at the same time. This was normal behaviour for them in the first month. It is important to mention that class sizes across the country are normally 30, and I had far fewer pupils than this, so they should have been easier to manage. Sadly, 16 of the pupils had what is known as a statement. This means some type of behavioural, emotional, social or learning need. In schools, this is normally highlighted via the school's online portal, which is used to monitor the data and academic history of each child. So in summary, my highly pragmatic thoughts were simplified into a basic methodology:

> *"If they cannot behave appropriately, learning ain't happening!"*

The biggest crime I've witnessed any school committing is accepting poor behaviour from pupils. If this happens as the norm, I would argue that the leaders are partly to blame for the social failure of the human beings they are serving, but mostly the blame rests on the headteacher. Many heads I have worked under have been weak in this area, and they haven't supported their staff. Sometimes I've asked myself how certain headteachers have reached that position. I will never know. We must, however, remember that children have pushed the boundaries for centuries. That is what children do, so there is no point being flabbergasted every time they misbehave, because we know they do this for fun. Boys, in particular, have brain chemistry that physiologically makes them take risks and get into more trouble. The key to eradicating, supporting and nurturing behaviour is to implement a series of effective and consistent consequences to poor behaviour, but also rewards for good behaviour, in order to level the process out. I believe we are not born to behave well or badly and it is our environment and how we are taught that creates us.

As an example, if I were to teach a less able class a highly complex task, such as quadratic equations, in week one of their academic year, what would be likely to happen? I assume probable failure, which would lead to obvious frustration, which would lead to straying off task, which would lead to more poor behaviour.

On the flip side, if I set work that was lower than their ability level, that would be showing them that I was conforming to low aspirations for them; meaning that successful outcomes would also be highly unlikely. So, my advice in any teaching context is that the level of the task you set should relate specifically to the ability of the group. Additionally, it is important to note that it is very common for highly intelligent pupils to misbehave, mostly due to boredom and lack of stimulation from the teacher or task.

So, in summary, before I even began to look at the maths provision for my class, I needed to understand the people in front of me, which is the same as it is in football. Regarding this group, one of my first strategies was to observe them with other teachers to see how they interacted in other subject areas. I then created a simple matrix of questions to help me work out how I could help myself, and therefore help them. These included:

- What makes them tick? Get distracted?
- What makes them work hard? Lose focus?
- What makes them succeed? Fail?

- What makes them behave? Misbehave?
- What makes them so demotivated? Motivated?
- What are their interests? What do they dislike?
- What are their strengths? Areas for development?
- What are they good at? Poor at?
- What makes them happy? Sad?
- What is their home life like? School life like?
- Who do they live with at home? Who are they friends with in school?
- Who do they work best with? Worst with?

How to glean the answers is down to the teacher's personal preferences, but examples include: pupil surveys, one-to-one mentoring, asking the previous class teacher of their experiences with the same group, but mostly spending time listening to them and asking how they feel about learning and life. Without this listening process, it is almost impossible to intervene accurately and teach with a style and approach that the class will understand. In my experience, the inability to listen is a key failure of many people. We were given two ears and one mouth for a reason.

> *I soon learnt that the core of the problem with this group was low self-esteem, both academically and socially. This key factor was causing the pupils to behave in extreme ways most of the time.*

Imagine spending five hours a day failing at stuff?

What impact would it have on your behaviour if you failed for that many hours a day? These young people were stuck together all day, every day as a bottom set class. Most had special educational needs of some sort, and the dynamics of the group simply didn't fit. I argued at the time with my peers on the leadership team that the school was failing these kids by labelling them in this way. But this is the politics of the education system, you see. School leaders make decisions that set kids up to fail all the time,

CHAPTER 27 - BEHAVIOUR MANAGEMENT OR BEHAVIOUR FOR LEARNING?

but no one says a word or challenges the status quo. Most teachers just moan about it on Twitter. I didn't have the power to change the overall strategy for this class, so all I could do was try my best to better their lives. I certainly would not have given them double maths for the last two lessons on a Friday, which is what happened! This is the graveyard shift in the educational domain!

What would the majority of leaders, managers, teachers or coaches do here?

The worst of them would probably blame the pupils. They would carry on labelling these young people unable, disaffected and disruptive, when the facts are that we, the leaders, had failed them. Day after day, year after year, the so-called experts are making poor decisions. It's shocking really. The people that are supposed to know how to lead people to success in life and inspire them are failing the so-called 'unteachable' children in every way, by setting them up to fail and putting them all together to rot. Another reason why I despise the placing of pupils into academic setting streams is that the less able groups, who find academia difficult, often display worse behaviour, which leads to lowering levels of progress for them as a whole.

However, there are many theories of strategy and solutions to support this issue. Many schools and elite sports clubs have used different approaches for years. It is important to note how it's often the case that initial questions need to be explored in order to find solutions and answers later on. One strategy is to place your best teacher or coach with your most able group. Now, I was one of the best regarding behaviour, but clearly I wasn't the best when it came to maths and geography.

Another theory is to put your best teacher or coach with your least able students. I remember hearing that Everton Football Club had all the academy staff on a six-week rotation for the differing age groups. This approach gives athletes access to many different types of coaching styles and personalities. That diversity can help, but on the downside it can hinder continuity and the relationships between learners and teachers. If you run a programme, that is for you to decide and reflect upon, as each method has its pros and cons.

There is a theory that you are only as good as your weakest link and not your strongest one, so if you are failing your bottom set pupils you are failing in general. I felt it was the school's duty to serve these children in a better way. Football clubs should be no different. They have an ethical and moral duty of care for all players. But does this always play out in sporting contexts? As a university lecturer, I mentored many trainee PE teachers by observing their lessons. Through this process, I got a varied overview of people's self-awareness, which was so often lacking. Often if lessons went horribly wrong, the trainee teacher would say, "Yes, that class was terrible. They are the worst class in the school!"

The blame culture and avoidance tactics had begun and they would use this poor behaviour as their get out clause. May I add that experienced teachers have also used this excuse. Nevertheless, in these situations, I was able to observe, judge and create in explicit detail a list of the real reasons why the classes were poorly behaved and struggling to learn and achieve. To put it bluntly, the blame had to be placed on the leader of the group – the teacher!

The main reason for these trends in poor quality lessons was normally one of the following:

- The teacher had poor subject knowledge, which led to inadequate learning outcomes. Often in teaching, this is one of the main reasons why pupils get bored and stray off task. The teacher simply hadn't got the knowledge to share, impart and inspire.

- The teacher is simply boring! They often have a boring and monotone voice and lack personality, which means the kids switch off completely. Harsh but true. Who wants a boring teacher?

- The teacher uses poor body language most of the time. Bad body language is rife in teachers and coaches who are below par. We talk about player body language, but what about the coaches? Arsene Wenger never got off his seat! I admire him greatly, but his negative body language certainly didn't help him. This is a priority to get right early on during teacher training. Not being able to see the class the entire time also means that additional poor behaviour will potentially occur, such as pupils nudging and kicking each other behind the teacher's back. In the schools I worked at, if you turned your back just the once there would be a punch to the back of the head going on somewhere.

- The activities and lesson structures are often disorganised, lack flow and are poorly planned.

I hope this has hit a nerve for both coaches and teachers, as the trained eye can spot a good and bad practitioner a mile off. I have witnessed poor behaviour and identified why it occurs for over 20 years. I hope my experience has enabled me to help you.

So, you see, it's not rocket science. It is basic human psychology. Understand your *own* behaviours before you try to understand other people's, and when those two processes synchronise and combine you will have hit the jackpot. I have always enjoyed using theoretical and historical research to back up my opinions. Below is a fantastic diagram, which I have always sworn by. Poor teachers and coaches do this a lot when they interact with people on a negative basis. It is called the *Betari Box*. Basically my advice is to never let someone's poor behaviour and attitude affect your own, so get thinking.

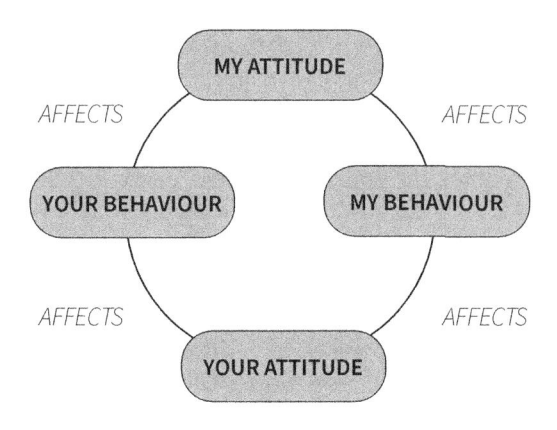

Figure 2. Betari Box.

Behaviour at Strategic Level

I want you to trust me on this. I once joined a school that was in the bottom 10% of schools in Britain. The standards of teachers, leadership, pupil behaviour and attainment had dropped to an all-time low. It had been placed in special measures, which meant that during an Ofsted inspection, the government educational advisors deemed the school to be failing. A new headteacher, Paul Petty, was put in place. He was actually my old deputy from a previous school, and this was his first headteacher's post. I was honoured to be on his hit list of the teachers he wanted to help raise standards as quickly as possible.

Paul had witnessed me first-hand in similar circumstances at our previous school, and he gave me the task of dealing with behaviour in the early part of my appointment. Although I thought this was one of my strengths as an educator, I am going to ask you to think about the following:

> - Why me, on my own? Could allowing me to deal with the majority of the behavioural issues have been a flawed approach towards sustained excellence?

I will talk about how to achieve sustained behavioural excellence, but first I want you to think about elite behaviours and if they are being displayed in your current team?

- If so, why? If so, how? If not, why not?
- What are the solutions to raising the bar for sustained behavioural excellence?
- Are the people in your institution aware of the objectives and targets you are trying to achieve regarding elite behaviours? If not, why not?

Remember, the above questions could be placed at the door of adults as well as children. After all, elite behaviours affect everyone. If you work with the correct people who are appointed in the right positions, productivity and performance will obviously improve. Paul's job was to recruit as many good and experienced staff as possible, in order to make this failing school a success again. He was a ruthless man, but he was also honest and demanded the highest standards from staff in the first instance.

The school was based in south east London and was surrounded by various deprived council estates. Like many London schools, it was unofficially linked to a gang and part of the improvement plan was to stop this affiliation as soon as possible. Behaviour at the school was simply unsafe, and the kids loved a punch up. Teachers were regularly assaulted, sworn at and threatened. We needed to act on this appalling conduct, of course, but first we had to understand our strategy for approaching these issues. The five-hour long meetings and brainstorming sessions amongst the senior staff made us fully aware that we needed to immediately implement policies to strengthen our strategy and support what we were trying to achieve on the coal face. In a nutshell, we were a truly passionate team, and we were dedicated to raising standards. I reiterate that we were a team and not a group. I believe there is a significant difference in the meaning of these two words. But the key question was: Where do you start in a school with so many issues?

Below, I've highlighted a simplified list of priorities, in order of importance.

1. **Assess the current skillset of the staff we have in the shortest possible time.** Once done, break them down into a RAG rating:

    - ✓ **Green** – Yes, we want to keep them and they are skilled.

    - ✓ **Amber** – Yes, we want to keep them, but they are underperforming so we need to support and upskill them, as they have lost their enthusiasm to work.

    - ✓ **Red** – The nos … No passion to stay, demotivated (but don't want to change) and low skill levels. Therefore, potential educational poison.

    In my experience, the biggest flaw of leaders or managers who enter a new job and fail is that they attempt to make *too many changes too soon*. Maybe this is because they feel the need to prove their worth early on in their appointment, but often it will come back to bite them on the backside if their assessment of the changes required was not accurate. However, a balance was needed on this occasion, because we didn't really have time on our side. School behaviour was getting worse by the day. So, just to put this into context, this was a drastic situation, and therefore a different model of management was required.

2. **Deal with the behaviour of unruly pupils with a zero tolerance approach, while adopting and incorporating high aspirations for them.** Aspirations are the key to institutional improvement, whether that's in a school or a football club. Secondly, it is a well-known fact in education that you cannot have an effective sanctions (punishment) policy if you don't support it with the more important rewards policy. Years of research has shown that rewarding good behaviour is equally as important as sanctioning poor behaviour. I once had a frank conversation with Dave Livermore about our philosophy around punishing players that were late for match day. My advice was clear. In order not to ruin the positive atmosphere of the pre-game routine for the rest of the squad, I explained that any manager should start his team talk with rewarding the players who turned up on time and ignoring the late comers (but addressing them with a sanction at a later date). That way, it keeps the mood good and positive pre-match. Lateness isn't ideal, but it happens, so using the Betari Box would be helpful here. Apply it!

3. **Punctuality, uniform and attendance** – Quite simply, you can't have any expectations of people if you don't get the basics right, i.e. the kids were told from day one that they had to turn up to school every day, turn up to school on time and wear the correct uniform all day, every day. They were then fully informed of the consequences if they chose to ignore these rules.

4. **Listen to your community** – You may be wondering what on earth this means and why it's important, but let me explain. Concerning the demographics of our school, we were in the heart of a London suburb. The community, i.e. shopkeepers and residents, detested the

school. They couldn't hide their anger at how often our pupils were destroying the area and interfering with their day-to-day lives. We had to address this quickly and understand that our progress relied not just on what went on in the school buildings (zooming in), but also the outside (zooming out). In summary, in order to change the school, we had to innovate against the norms and change the community with a genuine strategy rather than made-up rules.

I once studied the work of Robert Rosenthal, a psychologist, and Lanore Jacobson, a school principal (1968), among others, and they argued that teacher expectations influence student performance. In summary, they proved that positive expectations influence performance positively, and negative expectations influence performance negatively (Golem effect). They described this phenomenon as the *Pygmalion effect*.

> "When we expect certain behaviours of others, we are likely to act in ways that make the expected behaviour more likely to occur."
> (Rosenthal and Babad, 1985)

So, in summary, in terms of teaching and coaching:

- Staff who moan about students (the happy hoovers) establish a climate of failure.
- Staff who value their students' abilities create a climate of success (happy hairdryers).

Here are some more questions for you to consider:

- What kind of learning climate are you creating through your expectations when you teach or coach?
- What are your colleagues like? Do they influence people with a positive or negative culture?
- Are your colleagues professional at all times or do they undermine all the good work with pessimistic mindsets, unprofessional

conversations with the children and negative approaches to practices by displaying poor body language and many other negative behaviours?

My advice? Whatever your answers are to these questions, address them! Kids want good teachers and coaches, *not* mates!

If you teach and coach well, they will like you anyway!

CHAPTER 28

Elite Athletes and Resilience... Born, Made or Destroyed?

"A person who never made a mistake, never tried anything new."
– Albert Einstein

This may sound autocratic and draconian, but often in my teaching days as a school leader, the harsh side of my persona emerged when I had to tell inadequate teachers that maybe the education industry wasn't for them, and that they should think about another career. May I add that these very difficult conversations came after months and sometimes years of support. This process included mentoring and coaching interventions for staff members who really needed help. Sadly, even after all this assistance, they still consistently implemented a profligate teaching strategy.

To put it bluntly, many of these educated professionals, some of whom had first-class degrees from top universities, were not cut out for a career as a teacher. Having degree-level teaching qualifications was one thing, but these people often lacked the resilience, skills and diligence to stick it out through the rough times in schools, and trust me it really was tough. I would like to emphasise they were not bad people, but simply not up to the task in a tough industry that requires serious desire, application and high skill levels.

However, as mentioned earlier, the support networks available to them were thorough and through various line management procedures, I would often ask the weaker teachers if they thought they were suited to a career in education. I then questioned their response in detail. Sadly, the truth is – and it's similar in elite sport – teaching is not for everyone. It's a hardcore job and if it were easy everyone would do it for the 13-week holidays (and the even longer ones in the private sector).

So, what is more important, ability, resilience or effort?

With regards to resilience and effort in sport, I believe it is a fine line when youth athletes start to play at an elite level in their mid-teenage years. Roger Federer was famously quoted as saying, "Sometimes you're just happy playing. Some people, some media, don't understand that it's OK to play and actually just enjoy playing tennis. They always think you have to win everything."

I believe that many academy coaches need to rein themselves in a bit on occasion, and remember what they are there for. They must regularly remind themselves that sport at junior level is to be enjoyed and that is all it is for, even at elite junior level. Here's some more advice: elite youth athletes need to think about themselves and what their aspirations are a lot sooner. They need to deeply reflect and think about their *future self* sooner rather than later. The problem is, of course, that if you ask a young person to reflect they either think you're mad and old, or they go straight to the mirror and put on some hair gel!

I firmly believe that this reflective process would not only help athletes understand themselves better and earlier in their lives, but it would greatly help them to perform in the sport they have chosen to pursue as a potential career. Additionally, it would be a welcome strategy in the short, medium and long-term for the athlete to think about what they do well and what they need to do to improve. This type of deeper thinking will support their future self both in and out of the sport and warn against any potential rejection in the coming years. After all, rejection in life is common, so my advice to young athletes is rather blunt, and it's to get used to it early! The balance is using the Pygmalion effect with a personal approach. Every athlete is unique, so it's important to be honest about their strengths and limitations.

It makes me laugh when I think about how for many decades, headteachers, particularly primary school ones, put a ban on winning at school sports days. I mean, really! What rubbish. Winning and losing is a massive learning curve, and learning about losing early in life is only going to make people stronger in the long-term. Forget sport here, this is lifelong learning. I just wish that parents across the globe would understand the process of building resilience more efficiently, and not always look for short-term gain by falsely protecting their children against failure. As the saying goes, "Short-term pain for long-term gain."

However, I need to put the next question to you all:

> - Can a young person *be taught* to have hunger and desire as they go from their teenage years into adulthood?

I personally believe their hunger and desire can be improved and nurtured, but I also feel that any intervention needs to be implemented before the age of about 10. In some cases, however, athletes need a different strategy and may require nurturing and possibly a softer approach to building resilience. It needs to be noted that, in my experience, elite coaches often perceive the more sensitive athletes as weak before they are given the chance to become strong. This is because it takes a trained brain to understand that strong can be seen in different ways within human behaviour. For those who are involved in youth development, bear in mind that none of us have a crystal ball about the perfect development journey and it annoys me when people think that it is concrete and fixed in its creation or pathway. Therefore, whatever level you work at, I advise you to be a chameleon in your approach to athlete development and connect your aspirations to the standard of the players you work with. As mentioned previously, success and winning is brilliant, but every team and athlete has a ceiling point on how much they can achieve. Maybe that will serve as a little reminder to the Sunday league managers out there who scream, shout and talk crap after every defeat. Simply reward the progress and effort these kids make. That is all you need to do.

My first school consisted of 2,600 pupils. Put simply, it was pretty easy to win the London or District Cup. Why? Because we had the most pupils out of any school in the City of London, so the law of averages meant we would have a good team. Many boys from the school went on to play games in the football league, including Junior Stanislas (West Ham), Michael Turner (Charlton Athletic) and Ben Chorley (Arsenal). However, at my second school, the standard of the kids was much lower and therefore the expectations from myself and for the department had to change. Losing 4-0 was often seen as a success for many teams. As I said previously, you have to put your aspirations in the context of the athletes' abilities. The two have to be entirely synchronised.

Have you ever thought about the differences between recreational sport and elite sport in youth participation?

Let me tell you, it is vast in every way. In many respects at youth level, I believe it is harder for a young athlete to perform outside the elite environment. Why? Because lower down the sporting ladder the education and knowledge of the parents and coaches is often not as high, and sadly the parents want to win more than the kids do. Across the UK, it is well known in the football sphere that parental conduct is potentially at its worst and putting serious and unnecessary pressure and stress on children. On a typical Sunday morning on a football field in South London, I have heard all sorts of rubbish and nonsense being shouted at children, which has no relevance to learning and resilience whatsoever. And in case you haven't read correctly, these are children. Basically, I call this type of behaviour child abuse. It is wrong and has to stop.

As the experts, we talk regularly to players about emotional control, but often parents and coaches are the worst at exercising it. And explaining this to them is almost impossible, as their appalling behaviour doesn't make them self-aware enough to listen or change. Additionally, in the elite environment, some of the coaches and parents at pro clubs need to have a word with themselves about using shouting and screaming as the only way to convey their messages. I am the loudest man ever on the sideline, but I use the loud voice tool only when I need to, and not as a matter of course.

Here's a great quote from former Millwall Lionesses coach, Dan Logue:

> *"You wouldn't shout at a young person for not being able to read very well, so why would you shout at them if they make a bad pass in a football match or hit a bad shot at tennis?"*

So, think about this: What's the difference between learning to read a book and learning to play sport? The bullet points below, although no doubt very obvious to most people, are four basic elements of skill acquisition and are linked to both reading and sport:

1. The need to understand what the teacher/coach and the learner need to do in order to be successful, e.g. talking through the learning journey and looking at what is required to improve.

2. How we/you are going to achieve it, e.g. how to read, how to pass the ball well.

3. Breaking down the skill journey into parts, e.g. planting their non kicking foot/reading a word before a sentence or pronouncing the sound of the word.

4. Hours of good quality practice and repetition.

As you can see, learning is learning at the end of the day and often it does not need to be complicated. In many respects, I believe less is more and the best educators simplify everything. Another one of Jimmy Bullard's qualities was the repetition of, "Sallis, keep it simple, simple, simple, my son." From experience, some teenage athletes often feel that they have to keep playing sport due to various issues outside of their own requirements and needs. Parental pressure is a common one. Motivation often dwindles going into the teenage years, as various external influences take over, which, as we all know, can make many young people lose focus.

Now, let me ask you this:

- Do you think my previous statement is accurate?
- Have some coaches and parents killed motivation for youngsters, before it has even had a chance to grow?

We know that teenagers' motivation diminishes for various reasons, so please take a hard look at the young athletes you serve and ask them why this is so. Have you actually asked them this question lately? Something like, "What do you enjoy about me being your coach, the sport itself, training and matches?"

I urge you to make an impact with these questions at the various levels of performance you work at, whether that's elite level or lower down towards amateur standard. In fact, the standard does not matter. Elite athletes need to be educated about how to enjoy their sport too. The best coaches promote this. The worst are often so tense themselves that everyone loses.

In the modern world, life opportunities and education pathways are more diverse and effective, so for many athletes, young and old, a career in sport isn't everything to them. As an example, the England cricketer, Zafar Ansari, left the sport in 2017 to pursue a career in law. A colleague of mine, Chris McCready, who played professional football for many years at Crewe, has done some great work and research across the country on this topic for his PhD. We speak regularly and his research suggests that there is no simple answer to why athletes often leave professional sport. However, it is clearly not for them. But what about the flip side to this argument and the players that have only one destiny in life, and that is to play sport for a job? Let's not forget that over the decades, many of the world's sports stars have been highly successful due to a few common trends:

- Deprivation as a child
- Living in poverty
- Seeing sport as their only way out

In contrast, Olympic sport throws up some different statistics that show the majority of British Olympians are privately educated (which explains why they tend to dominate the GB team at international events). The statistics say that roughly 70% have had a non-state education. So, whatever their background, a born hunger for sporting success has somehow transferred itself into the make up of all successful athletes. I said at the beginning of this book that I would pose as many questions as I did answers. So, what do you think about the philosophy regarding hunger and resilience for athletes?

CHAPTER 28 - ELITE ATHLETES AND RESILIENCE...BORN, MADE OR DESTROYED?

- Are athletes born, made or even destroyed?
- Does their/your environment make or break them?
- Do parents negatively affect their children's sporting chances or help them achieve?
- Are the elite-level coaches as good as they are perceived to be?
- As an educator, how truly holistic is your programme and philosophy?
- Do you actually know what holistic really means and how it feels for the athletes?

I'll let you decide...

CHAPTER 29

Sport Psychology: What is it?

"We all bullet point our triumphs, but I am who I am because of everything you don't see on my CV. The stuff that doesn't work out teaches you how to trust your instincts and adapt." – Aimee Mullins

My work as a physical education specialist has been linked several times to sport psychology. In fact, its very origins go back to the German physical education colleges that existed in the 1920s. There are many crossovers in history between education, psychology and sport, and so this story continues.

It all stems from a culture!

At the end of my first season at Millwall, I went down the pub with the rest of the academy staff. We proceeded to discuss where we were at with regards to the quality of our under-18 scholarship programme. We used a simple self-assessment method that day:

- W.W.W. (What Went Well)
- E.B.I. (Even Better If)

Essentially, we discussed the good things about what we were trying to achieve with the programme, and what we needed to develop and improve on as a team. The previous week, I'd handed some anonymous questionnaires to the 20 or so players enquiring about their thoughts and feelings towards the scholarship programme. Mostly I asked for general comments, but some questions could open us up to be challenged. Something I have learnt over many years is that self-awareness is key in the journey to successful leadership. From experience, what many so-called education and coaching experts fail to recognise is that the people they serve (the players and students) may have many feelings about them that are not expressed, or, more importantly, aren't listened to due to suppressive regimes. This is mainly due to one single emotion, and that's fear.

So, going back to the story I was telling you about, the next item on our loosely written agenda, which was scribbled on a dirty napkin (yes, you read that correctly, we worked on an agenda from the pub garden), was entitled, 'Sport psychology intervention.' The current strategy we had concerning psychology was rather blatantly 'in progress'. In other words, we simply didn't have one.

However, as I would often put to the staff, did we *really need* an intervention?

We had previously discussed the topic over the season and regularly differed in our opinions. As usual, I was probably overt in my opinions, which is never a surprise to my colleagues, past or present, as I am not shy about sharing my passion. I claimed that although a specific psychology intervention may help and add value to our programme, I wasn't convinced it was a necessity to help us produce professional footballers. In support of my argument, remember that I had come from big schools, with one having nearly 3,000 kids in the building. Let me tell you, that was a full-on task! On the other side of the coin, we only had 18 players to deal with. My rationale to not requiring or needing a sport psychologist will be explained later in this chapter, and in better detail.

I worked alongside the two under-18 managers, Dave Livermore and Justin Skinner, the physio Adam Johnson, the sports scientist Paul Stretch, the head of video analysis Nick Donger Hicks, and the head of goalkeeping, Sebby Barton. I must emphasise that we were a very tight team professionally. In fact, I would say they were the most cohesive group of people I have ever worked with. A huge part of our success was our passion for excellence and our regular ability (if you can call it that) to disagree. Yes, you heard it, we disagreed all the time, but the key to our success was that we never held grudges. That was the magic gold dust, to be honest. Emotionally, we were a tight bunch and cared about each other personally as well as professionally. Four years later, we're still in a WhatsApp group together.

Now, you may wonder how we got to that stage. And you may be reading this and thinking about the people that you work with and how this type of unity wouldn't be possible. But think about it more deeply. If this is the case, why is it not achievable? In the past, I often worked with people who got majorly offended if someone disagreed with them, and in turn this would cause long-term factions within the group. I believe this type of insecurity in people can become problematic.

As a group, we would discuss our goals throughout the season, and we were generally similar in our thoughts and feelings. Put simply, we wanted to create a 'sustainable, aspirational and high-achieving model' that would produce professional athletes for 10 years rather than 10 months. We would often emphasise that success was not about getting players into the first team so they could just play a few games, as had happened historically. We wanted to create players for a sustained five-hundred game career, and to help mould a holistic athlete with a solid lifestyle who portrayed elite behaviour, had a great attitude when it came to learning and the intrinsic dedication needed for success both on and off the pitch.

As a team of staff, we held the similar view that the person behind the player was a key focus for successful outcomes and the development of the athlete's character was a priority. We had some potentially tricky players in the squad that season, who we had managed to collectively turn around from potentially dysfunctional individuals to selfless and articulate success stories. The saying, "Like hangs around with like" was very pertinent for us, as the few disruptive players didn't really have a choice in the end. They ended up being the odd one out if they chose to remain difficult and stay a dickhead.

> "The more we produced good people, the more chance we had of accelerated learning due to exceptional conduct from the whole squad."

The more the players behaved well, the more we could focus on the important stuff, such as the players' learning journey, rather than the usual nonsense that often happens at many football clubs, which is regular low-level disruption, poor conduct and players dicking about. So, without having to deal with poor culture all day we could focus on creating better performance outcomes for everyone involved, including the staff. We believed that if the staff weren't motivated and didn't care, there would be no hope of the players winning and becoming successful. Conduct, culture and behaviour was therefore our priority, and as long as I am involved in elite sport it always will be. I can't emphasise enough: If behaviour isn't explicitly good, how can learning be achieved?

Agree or disagree? You tell me, because in 20 years in education, I am yet to see it. In my experience, the downfall of coaches and teachers is either:

A. They disregard the conduct of the players and don't think of it as a priority.

B. They don't know and understand what exceptional conduct looks like, which means they are unable to address it.

C. They fail to understand the correlation between exceptional athlete behaviour and conduct, winning matches and happy people.

D. They focus too much on the calibre (technical and tactical) and not the character of the players (mindset).

The model I've created is very simple:

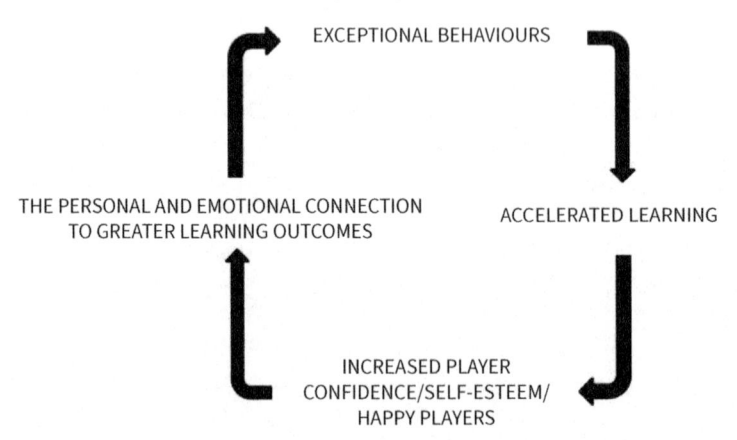

```
              EXCEPTIONAL BEHAVIOURS

THE PERSONAL AND EMOTIONAL CONNECTION        ACCELERATED LEARNING
   TO GREATER LEARNING OUTCOMES

              INCREASED PLAYER
           CONFIDENCE/SELF-ESTEEM/
                HAPPY PLAYERS
```

Figure 3. Sallis Square of Elite Behaviours

CHAPTER 29 - SPORT PSYCHOLOGY: WHAT IS IT?

> *As Joe Dumars, from the Detroit Pistons says, "On good teams, coaches hold players accountable, on great teams players hold players accountable."*

We believed the changing room had to drive the culture, even at youth team level. So referring back to the sport psychologist debate, I believed we simply did not need one. Dave strongly thought we did. Now, it was not uncommon for us to disagree. And I was not saying I was right and he was wrong, even though we were both passionate about our views. Additionally, I wasn't saying I didn't think a sport psychologist would be able to add value to the squad at some stage. But my stance was the following: What impact would a sport psychologist have if the entire squad or staff portrayed conduct that was listed as any of the following?:

- Unprofessional, tardy, no effort to train to the maximum, lack of cohesion.
- Hostile, aggressive behaviours, selfish.
- Players generally not knowing what good manners mean in and around the building.
- Players not seeing and valuing rules and therefore regularly breaking them.
- Staff failing to see the value in the above.

So, to give my argument more substance, it was also based around the following. I believed:

> *"Our sport psychology was everything we stood for."*

This included:

- How we made the players feel on a daily basis. (Building confidence, etc.)
- How we showed we cared with acts of selflessness and kind words.

- How we were ultra-professional as staff (organised, prepared, skilled, enthused to help the players in performance and non-performance related issues, etc.).
- Our daily standards (timekeeping, attitude to learning, demands on ourselves and players).
- Our rewards and sanctions policy (players knowing the rules with no grey areas and being rewarded for good behaviour).
- Mutual respect as a core driver of our culture.
- Using the Pygmalion effect every minute of every day.
- Differentiating the needs of each player in line with the four corner model.
- Daily staff conversations about each player, and with each player one-to-one.
- Monitoring the progress of players with complete rigour, so that they understood exactly where they were in their learning journey and, most importantly, what they needed to do to improve.

I appreciate that these points are simplified, but in my eyes that is sport psychology, particularly in terms of a larger, more scaled-up culture. I love the term 'paralysis by analysis'. Sometimes, coaches overanalyse everything. There is a lot to be said for bringing it right back to basics and making people feel emotionally safe and good every day, while being challenged to aspire to greatness.

In my opinion, this is what clubs need to recognise. It's not about someone coming in with a magic mental wand and expecting to charm players' minds into all of the above. It just does not happen. How do I know this? Because of working in schools, where being an expert in social psychology is standard practice for any great teacher, as is knowing how to be effective when faced with various stressful scenarios during the working day. I had a man come into school once and threaten to shoot me with a gun. It was past school hours, about 5pm, and he was wearing a long trench coat and was heavily drugged up and aggressive. Fortunately, after the police had been called from the special alarm the school had put in place, which linked them directly to police HQ in Lewisham, the man was arrested and it was discovered the gun was a replica. But how was I to know? I thought I was bang in trouble – another crazy moment in my life.

I have worked with educational psychologists closely for years. To put it bluntly, they can only be truly effective when the school sees their input as valuable and this is already embedded in their culture. Once a sound philosophy is rooted, you may have a chance with these specialist individuals. Now, another saying that is highly relevant to me is one I mentioned in Chapter 27. It goes as follows:

You are only as good as your weakest link and not your strongest one.

The meaning of the statement is this: It does not matter who you have in the building, whether it be staff or players, unless everyone contributes to all of the above. If you have a weak staff member you are basically stuffed, just like a school would be. In a big business, weaker people get saturated by the masses, and can go unnoticed, but in small teams they become more obvious. Now, the word weak is subjective, as is how this trait may come across. So, let me put this into context for you. Many of the people I have worked with are equally qualified. That is sadly the nonsense about qualifications. All these people I am about to mention are:

- Doctors
- Teachers
- Coaches
- Psychologists

But life isn't played out on bloody paper! Of the above, some are outstanding, some are average and some are simply rubbish. Teachers, coaches, leaders and psychologists are no different. I mentioned earlier how many teachers are letting schools down with their lack of ability to help the children they serve, whether that is academically, pastorally, emotionally or behaviourally. On many occasions, the majority of pupils will literally ignore everything these teachers say to them. So, can you imagine the psychology and mindset of the teenagers who have these inadequate teachers? Often, pupils will have two or three of these garbage educators in any one day. They will regularly defy them, which in turn causes chaos in the building. Children are not stupid; they will know they are not getting a good deal from these teachers, so of course they will rebel, which is simply human nature. Sadly, this often has serious ramifications for the pupils. These include:

- Increased anxiety
- Increased stress behaviours
- Poor academic performance
- Worsened behaviour
- Lowered aspirations, which leads to poor outcomes
- More low-level disruption and potentially more fights

> *I swear by the saying below, and it's one I always try to share:*
> *"Every behaviour needs a consequence, good or bad."*

My advice is that ignoring the above statement is going to end in tears. For the child, as well as for you.

Further evidence to back up my sport psychology theory involves a series of incidents I witnessed at a well-known professional club that has had persistently poor player conduct for several years. I have seen players rip their shirt off and throw it at staff after being subbed and tell their manager to fuck off. In a different game several months later, the same club had an entire squad of under-18 players answering back to the coaching staff, some of whom were very senior academy staff. This club has a full-time sport psychologist in its ranks, and from the latest statistics, has one of the worst records of players reaching first-team level in their respective leagues, along with poor education results for their scholars. Please don't think for a minute that I am placing the blame on the sport psychologist, but is it not obvious? What impact is one person going to have on a shambles culture if the football club's senior staff do not address it themselves and carry on accepting poor standards without intervention?

Similarly, the same rule applies in education. What can one exceptional teacher achieve with a load of rubbish teachers around that consistently and negatively influence teenagers for the other 90% of the time? The answer is obvious. Not a lot! All they do therefore, is fight other people's fires. Before people think I am sport psychology bashing, I am not. In fact, I have been offered to study a PhD in it. I'm simply trying to get people to understand that institutional change, whether that's in a football club, academy, business or school, will not happen unless the culture is absolutely bulletproof. No one person, whether that's a coach, manager, physio or psychologist, has a hope in hell of being effective if the systems, protocols and culture are poor. I am relentless about this. You really have no hope. Once this is embedded, individual intervention via mentoring and psychology is massive.

In summary, I have three final points to make about my experiences:

1. A qualification in a certain subject does not mean you are any good! (Sorry, but it's true.) This includes football, psychology and education. If this were the case, every doctor, teacher and coach would be amazing. And the reality is that they are not. So, what is the difference between a good and bad so-called expert? Answer: It's simple and it's down to their behaviour and actions rather than their qualifications.

2. I genuinely do think that a sport psychologist could add value to a programme. I mean this without question. But I have heard coach after coach say, "We need one, we need one, Steve!" I partially agree but:

    - Only if they are of exceptionally high quality and have a proven track record. This includes experiences that are not out of a textbook or university lecture theatre (note my sarcasm).

- If they enter an already solid, highly functioning programme, which everyone buys into. It's no good if half the team think they are helpful if the other half undermine the process when they walk through the door on day one. Football is an industry that traditionally lacks open-minded people in the first place. I believe this has negatively affected football compared to other sports. We have all been given a mind, but there is no point in having one if we are not going to use it effectively!

3. Of course, I understand that sport psychology is far more complex than I have explained and provides support in various ways, including in the fields of neuroscience, stress, anxiety, arousal, goal setting, self-talk, confidence, commitment, communication and imagery techniques, to name but a few.

Now, back to my original story. Six months later, Livers and I were driving to a player conference when he said, "Stevo, you know what, mate, I've been reflecting. You were correct back then regarding what you said in the pub about how sport psychology is what we do every day, and that there is no magic wand. But with our rigour for excellence, with pathways towards aspiration and demanding player interventions which show kindness, selflessness and an openness to listen to our players, I truly believe anything is achievable. You helped me understand that this is in reality the key factor that determines the mindset of our players."

> *And this is what I call sport psychology. It is a culture where: All the staff give the players the best possible platform to perform as highly as they can for as long as they can.*

And in the long term, it's where players can hopefully seek out the performance and life solutions for themselves.

SECTION FIVE
The Final Whistle – The Power of Parents – Good and Bad.

This section of two chapters looks into parental involvement in sport and how mums and dads can help but also hinder their children.

CHAPTER 30

The Secret Parents: Trials and Tribulations

"In order to be successful you must prepare for the unexpected – and I wanted to prepare them for that." – Richard Williams, father of Venus and Serena Williams. When asked why he let his girls be exposed to abuse on court, he replied, "Criticism can bring the best out of you."

This chapter follows the stories of two sporting parents whose children are involved at elite level. The first one is with regards to a boy from a premier league football club. His account is split into two parts – pre and post his fourteenth birthday. The second story recounts the experiences of the parent of a youth county cricket player.

The secret parent – Story 1/Part 1: Pre 14 years

It had been a long day. We'd covered more miles and I'd been left wondering: Is this what I want? Is this what my son wants? Is it all worth it? It wasn't unusual for there to be tears in the car. Ever since my son was nine, the pressure I had heaped on him as he took the journey through the academy system had been confusing for him and often unbearable for me. It was undoubtedly painful for all of the people who cared about us both.

Today, though, there was a difference. The tears were mine. We were not on our way back home from a game and nitpicking about what he could or should have done – today marked the beginning of a new journey, the start of a period that he and I had been pushing for seven years. At the age of 16, he was moving away from home and I was dropping him off to live with another family, as he started his two-year professional scholarship.

Of course, I'd known this was coming. He had been offered the scholarship when he was 14 and had committed to it then, but this did not make it any easier and, as I drove away with tears in my eyes, I wondered for a second what it would be like to have the normal father and son relationship that had been taken away from us the second he showed he was exceptionally talented at the wonderful game I had grown up with – football. I was asking myself a lot of questions, rhetorically, of course, especially concerning whether this was the best course of action for him (and me). How did the rest of his family – his brother and his mum – feel? I questioned what we had all given up, why we had done it and if it had been worth it. If it all ended tomorrow, would my son see all this as wasted time and a wasted childhood, or would he look back and view it as a wonderful period of his life? There were many questions without any answers. I am not sure I can ever answer those questions, and I don't think he can either, not until the day he is released and is unable to make a living playing football, or he is looking back and reflecting on his football career.

OK, I am not going to second guess how my son feels about all this. What I will try to do is articulate some of my feelings about the last seven years; the highs and the lows, the praise and the criticism of the system, the club, the game and maybe even myself.

What I would like to state categorically from the outset is that I wanted my son to play football. What father doesn't? From the moment he showed talent, I wanted him to be signed to an academy, and to push himself and to be pushed. Why? I had experienced it myself (in a very out-dated way many moons ago!). I knew it wasn't going to be nice and relaxed. I knew how hard it was. Did I want him to succeed where I had failed? Yes, probably. What dad doesn't? I knew I was exposing him to a world of jealousy, bitching, backbiting and egomaniacs, and that's just the touchline and the parents! But I could also tell from an early age that my son was competitive, and that he thrived on it.

The day I first saw my son put on the kit of a professional football club was easily one of the proudest days of my life. He was nine. He had been on trial for three weeks and, having shown he was at the required level, he was selected for games and given the opportunity to show that he was better than the boys they had already signed. From there on in began the rollercoaster of ups and downs, and to be honest it never ended. I already felt a little frustrated about what I'd witnessed. I have coached to a reasonable level and have the same qualifications as many academy coaches. I'd played to a good, non-league level and much higher than a lot of them, too. Great, would you not think? I could enjoy this, couldn't I? Wrong. It was a curse. Training nights were not about chatting and bonding with the other parents while we enjoyed watching our little heroes show more talent than any of us had ever possessed. No, it was torture. It was like being Moses and watching someone else set light to a tree, or Noah visiting the shipyard. I was analytical and critical to the extreme – of everyone and everything. I watched every single thing my son did; I saw every mistake, every lapse in concentration, every moment of laziness, every weakness and every bad decision. What's worse is that I saw all this through the eyes of a 40-something ex player and coach, and sadly not through the eyes of a nine-year-old boy who had only been playing the beautiful game for 24 months. And I wanted to talk about it the minute he got into the car for the entirety of our 45-minute drive home. It did not end there, either. This curse of having experience and knowledge led me to being just as critical of the poor guy coaching my son. It made me critical of the academy system in general and it made me critical of the club he belonged to. Yes, I was a cynical father.

Right or wrong? *Wrong*, I hear you say.

Well, it's not as easy as that. Was I wrong to expect our academy system to be better than the rest of us, and the grassroots club I knew? The academy wanted the best players and they wanted to be able to be brutal in their judgement of these boys. Why then should they be exempt from the same expectations of excellence from us parents? I wanted my son to receive the best coaching, the best advice and the best environment, and it frustrated me when I felt he wasn't getting it. I discovered quite quickly that the system, the clubs and the coaches did not want to be judged in the same manner as they judged the players. They didn't like it when they were questioned about their methods. Doing so did not help my popularity and at times it did not help my son, either.

My boy signed academy forms as a nine year old, to play U10s football. He had stood out from the crowd, along with two or three other boys from the current team he had played with for a couple of seasons. I was constantly shocked by the number of boys from other teams his age that had been on trial at the same professional club without anyone so much as noticing the lads he was playing with for his Sunday outfit. The professional scouts were simply inadequate at the time. It was beyond belief really. His Sunday side were exceptional, with quality players throughout. Eventually, however, no fewer than seven of them were signed by different professional clubs, but for some reason the local scouting network had ignored them for ages.

My son had a pretty uneventful first couple of seasons in his new elite environment. Having been fortunate to be signed along with two other boys from the same Sunday team, I was able to share the burden of travelling with the other parents, though I never really had a problem with that. I liked going to other grounds and seeing him in new environments. As we grew more comfortable, it made us feel rather special. My son was among the top players in his age group in the country and the more I saw of the other boys, the more I realised he wasn't out of place.

However, it wasn't long before I started to see some cracks. Not with my own son, as he was very fortunate in that he seemed well thought of, but there were definitely issues with his teammates. His close friend, a skilful winger, was slowly having his confidence drained, as he was played out of position regularly, firstly as a centre forward and then many other positions. To this day, we think the coach thought he was my son, who was a centre forward. It wasn't that he failed in new positions, or that he wasn't a good player. It wasn't even a problem being asked to rotate positions now and again, it was simply that he hated playing there and the lack of consistency affected his mindset. He didn't enjoy his football anymore.

The Secret Parent – Story 1/Part 2: Post 14 years

The phone rang. It was the academy manager.

I had my usual thought: What have I done wrong? By this stage, I had worked at the club on and off in a small capacity: first as a scout, then

CHAPTER 30 - THE SECRET PARENTS: TRIALS AND TRIBULATIONS

later as a coach. There was always something I had done wrong. I'd said the wrong thing, Tweeted the wrong thing, updated my Facebook status without their approval.

"Can you come in tomorrow for a chat?"

"Why? What have I done now?" I said with my tongue firmly in my cheek.

"No, nothing like that," the manager said.

As I approached the stadium with my son, I checked with him that he had not done anything wrong. He assured me there was nothing. By then he was 14 and he had been doing well. He was regularly one of the best players on the pitch and it was not unusual for opposition parents and coaches to comment positively. I was beginning to feel less anxious. Something told me this was going to be a good meeting.

My feelings were confirmed when other staff greeted us with smiles and handshakes. It was as if they wanted to be part of the scene and feel like they'd contributed. However, they hadn't. They just wanted to pretend to themselves they had. Typical football coaches, eh? From day one, the majority of the coaching at the club had been dire. There were exceptions, of course, and one or two were exceptional in recognising my son's talent, but overall the place was full of people who hadn't played the game and didn't understand kids. In my eyes, this was a bad combination for the people responsible for helping develop kids to progress. We were led to the academy managers' office. With him was my son's lead phase coach. We exchanged some fake smiles and pleasantries. I never felt easy in their company. Like many football people they were fake and insecure. I knew I was a good coach; I knew I was a good dad; I even knew I had the same qualifications as these people. Despite this, I always felt intimidated by them. They never got that. They never understood how hard it was for parents to talk to them or ask a question. They had zero soft skills. Often, they were all just front and ego.

They told you it was fine and that they wanted you to be open about your opinions and feelings, but they never understood how hard it was for you to do that. They didn't get your fear that questioning them might lead to them treating your son differently or lessening his chances of progressing. But maybe they did. Maybe they played on that fear to prevent parents from questioning their methods. I called this a 'God complex,' and I still do. They believed they were God. They were playing with children's lives and their dreams, and toying with the various emotions of the families they were supposed to serve and support. I saw parents wrestling with themselves and their hearts whilst attempting these conversations, knowing deep down it was the right thing to do for their son, while fighting the fear that the coach might take it out on their boy's future if they didn't like what was being said.

Back to the meeting. They were all smiles – it was fine this time. This was the part they enjoyed. Telling you that they'd done their jobs so well that they were going to offer my 14-year-old son his scholarship early and a contract that would take him through to the age of 18. They told my boy he was the youngest player in the club's history to be offered this type of deal. However, this wasn't true. Now, I am not a stupid person. I have been around the game. But at that moment I lost myself in a wave of pride and love for my child and forgot in an instant the one thing I knew better than anyone ... that these people only do what is best for them and what may benefit them the most. This was not about my son, this was about the other clubs that had shown an interest in him and their fear that they may lose an 'asset', albeit a 14-year-old prepubescent one.

What I heard next was, on reflection, an embarrassing, unjustified, ridiculous array of words that ranged from promises and predictions to pure lies.

I quote:

- "We need to accelerate you."
- "You will be fast-tracked through the system."
- "We see you like (Player A – an U16 currently in the 21s) and can push you on the same path."

And the best one:

> "When other players are signing their scholarships at 16, we will be tearing this up and discussing a pro deal."

He was set a couple of small targets:

- "An appearance for the 18s before the end of next season (U15s)." – He achieved that!
- "Regularly in the 18s squad as an U16." – He achieved that too!

Despite trying to play it cool and asking for time to think, we left the building on cloud nine. I will not lie – I smiled the entire journey home. Two weeks later, we put pen to paper on a pre-scholarship agreement for my son. But this turned out to be the worst decision I ever made for him. From that moment on, I never once felt he was important to that football club, apart from one moment when, as an U15, he received a call up for an England U15's training camp. Of course, the same people who had greeted us at the stadium a year earlier all smiles and wanting to be part of the glory were present again.

My son was regularly playing up an age group, but this came with its own problems. The U15s going into U16s were slowly falling by the wayside and, as their mates started dropping away, my son was subjected to many jealousies and much animosity over his scholarship. Did the staff back their judgement and show their belief in him? Did they stick to their word and continue to push him to fulfil his potential? Did they fast track him, accelerate him, make him the best he could be? Of course not, this is football, which involves loads of emotion, selfishness and poor leadership. Upon signing the pre-scholarship, the interest from the two big premier league clubs died a death. There was no reason to look after him now, as he was secured, which meant no one could touch him without a substantial fee being involved.

He was in and out the side, albeit playing up a year, which did nothing for his confidence or his relationships with the lads, who were jealous of him. He was starting as a sub or coming off early and he rarely played in the position that he considered his best. It frustrated him and it angered me. They say playing 'up' is the pinnacle. Not in this case.

I regularly asked the question about his development and, on reflection, I was lied to. At the time it was another case of feeling slightly intimidated by these people with their tracksuits and their club badge on their chests. I am angry now that I failed to say more, as this was my son's future after all. I had a right to ask and a right to expect honesty and to feel it was OK to talk to them about it, as you would with a schoolteacher, I suppose. The difference is that the football industry contains bigger egos. As I said earlier, they had a 'God complex' and made you scared to voice an opinion through fear of you exposing their ignorance. Parents also worried that voicing their point of view would affect their son's future.

My boy was played in different positions to help his 'all round game'. This made sense until it dawned on me that he was the only player doing this and that he rarely played in his preferred position. By the time he was a scholar he was still being played in alternative positions and I realised that this had become so regular that actually where he played was … anywhere! I did some analysis on it in his first year and found he spent 25% of his game time in his preferred position and 75% of it in the areas he hated playing in.

I was told once that he was on the bench "because he was secured and had his scholarship sorted so it was only fair to play the others and give them a chance to earn theirs". Well, that really was fast tracking him and accelerating his progress, wasn't it …

The contradictions and lies just kept coming. By the time he was trying to earn his pro deal, he was left out the side to accommodate the lads who were already pros, because they were pros and therefore above him in the pecking order! If he asked why he didn't play a certain position more often, he was left out the side and other players took his place. When he enquired why this had happened, he was told, "Well, you only want to play (in a certain position), don't you?" As a first year scholar, he was left out the FA Youth Cup side and told that the second year scholar he was equal to had been given preference, as this was his last chance in the Youth Cup. The

CHAPTER 30 - THE SECRET PARENTS: TRIALS AND TRIBULATIONS

following year he sat on the bench while five first-year scholars and two U16s played. Embarrassingly, they lost by several goals whilst thumped at home in the first game!

I wouldn't blame you for coming to the conclusion that my son was one of the weaker players. Well, he wasn't. He was a leading player in his age groups throughout his time at the club. From the U10s to U18s, he scored more than 180 goals – from midfield! He represented England and was put on standby for many other squads. Since the U12s he always played a year up, sometimes two years up. On a couple of occasions he also played three years up.

I honestly think (and fear) that my frustrations and, ultimately, my anger resulted in the changing treatment of my son. I admit that I wasn't great at going in and talking to them; I preferred to email or text. That is not ideal, I know, but it suited me and helped me to clarify my thoughts better and put forward my point of view without being talked over or have my points rubbished. But it also meant that I could end up saying too much or even demonstrating that I had a good understanding of the situation ... possibly sometimes an even greater understanding than they did.

I emailed one coach after an U16 game and criticised my son's performance and his work rate. I felt he had yet to develop in parts of his game and that the reason for this was that they repeatedly made him play in different positions. I pointed this out and also that their refusal to be honest with him over his performances had made him complacent and that he failed to even recognise that he could and should do better. One day, I got a reply with some statistics from the GPS data showing how hard he worked, to which I pointed out that you can rack up 11km in a game by walking round the centre circle and that this told us nothing about:

- Where he had run.
- Why he had run to certain areas.
- How often he had run or even if he had run at the right times.
- It also told us nothing about the times he hadn't run when he should have done, and vice versa.

I received a reply saying, "We are disappointed in your criticisms of the academy and the work we do here."

A few years earlier, during my son's schoolboy days, I emailed a coach to question why he was playing as a defender. I asked:

- What it was hoping to achieve?
- How or where he was developing? (I also questioned his playing time.)

A month later, my son had not figured much in games and was excluded from the latest England camp, with another player from the squad attending in his place. Coincidence? Maybe. Despite this, he continued to perform well. His player/parent reviews were always good. The club were consistently telling us that he was exceptionally talented in all areas of his game and that although they had players as good as him in each part, he was the only one that could "do it all".

The only consistent criticism of him was that his defending was not good enough. This would always come up. As a coach myself, I could understand this, but the focus was starting to swing too heavily in the direction of the staff worrying about this, which was to the detriment of his attacking attributes. I raised this once with the academy manager. He told me not to worry and that attacking was instinctive for him and would always come back and be a big strength. They continued to focus on his defending, but they never played him in a position to expose his weakness. The results were too important to allow him to develop.

I asked them several times to stop playing him in an area that hid his weakness, as he was showing no improvement in the one area they felt he needed to improve. I challenged them on several occasions to play him in an area that would force him to defend, and I was told they did not trust him enough. They failed to verify if this was true by trying him out, they just guessed. By his second year, he had tried so hard to please them and to defend better that the goals had dried up. The U23's manager told him he could not pick him as he was not impacting games going forward. You could not make it up. These experts really were failing to adhere to their status.

The writing was on the wall. They did not like him and they did not like me, with the second person in that statement clearly being the main problem, I believe!

My son was released at the end of his U18 year, but with Steve's help he has realised his potential and he is now playing regularly in league one.

The Secret Parent – Story 2

This is the journey of an academic and high-performing twelve-year-old youth cricketer, his sacrifices and an exhausted mother.

When I became a mother in 2005, I wasn't destined to be a 'sporting parent'. I admit, I definitely had, and continue to have, high expectations, but I never really dreamed I would become immersed in the world of youth sport.

The questions I now ask myself are:

- Was my eldest son destined to be high performing?
- Is nature or nurture the key to success?

I definitely believe the influence of a parent with high expectations has led my son to strive to be the best he can be, but I think he needed to have the talent in the first place. From what I have seen so far, I don't believe that hard work alone can push a child to the top of their field; they have to have the inner drive and passion themselves, as well as the appropriate physical and mental attributes.

I vividly recall how when my son was six, he was nominated to attend a Talent ID day for the LTA (Lawn Tennis Association). That's when I woke up as a 'sports parent'. What a responsibility! How exciting! What if he really does have talent? Wow! It was so exciting and his dad and I said to each other that we must explore how good he is. Most nights we rushed from school to tennis lessons. Most of our meals were eaten out of Tupperware containers in the car, and life was about chasing tennis tournaments and working out how many more wins were required to go up to the next grade. It was exhausting, exhilarating and often emotional. All his birthday and Christmas presents were to do with his kit; life at this stage was simply about one thing … tennis.

I researched Spanish training camps. We thought nothing of driving three hours each way for a week of training at Bisham Abbey National Sports Centre or taking him to The National Tennis Centre. These were inspiring environments and it was thrilling to be around such high performers. Nothing could beat the pride and emotion I would feel when he won a match, especially the tougher ones. I would hide my tears of pure love, pride and overwhelming disbelief that this was happening, and his wins became a major high for all the family. But with highs come lows, of course. Soon enough, we had the low; emotions ran high as my son, then aged eight, couldn't contain his disappointment at losing a tournament. He was right, his opponent had cheated and he was also right that it was unfair. But that is life and one of the great lessons of mini tennis.

My son made such a spectacle that the other parents were looking and commenting. Did I go and comfort him? No! That would add fuel to the fire. Eventually, when he came to me, I commented on his behaviour and asked, "Why are we doing this? You are meant to be having fun!"

That was the last time he chose to play tennis for several years. It was heartbreaking, as he was talented, but at that point in his life, he didn't have the mental resilience required to carry on.

In the meantime, his rugby and cricket interests and skills were developing. Whatever he played he would say it was 'training' and he'd get really upset if the other children didn't take the sport seriously. It was never about having some fun on a Sunday morning for a few hours – he wanted to play with the more skilled players and be picked for the 'A teams'. Come rain or snow, he always attended rugby training. At one stage, he played in a national rugby tournament with a broken thumb. He wanted to be involved, even though he wasn't fully fit. I loved seeing his hunger and commitment and watching him enjoy himself.

CHAPTER 30 - THE SECRET PARENTS: TRIALS AND TRIBULATIONS

Cricket gathered momentum and his great eye-hand coordination was soon noticed. Being a left arm bowler also attracted much interest. Maximising his potential required quality training, and wasn't just about chasing the 10,000 hours of practice, which is so widely lauded and often referenced. He needed coaching that was engaging and that stretched and challenged him. In terms of the coach, he required someone who could create an emotional connection and the eye to spot and nurture his talent. He attracted much attention and played in older teams before being selected for district cricket, and then county cricket for Surrey at the age of nine.

More time passed and his enjoyment of all sport was evident, which made me realise how important it was for us to ensure that his senior school offered quality sports coaching in a high-achieving environment. My son wanted to be surrounded by other high performers who thought like him. He had that academically, but he was outgrowing the sporting provision of his current environment.

This led to us making the life-changing decision to move 200 miles so our son and his brother could attend a school famous for its sporting excellence. My husband and I didn't need much persuading, because as soon as we visited the school we felt we were in an environment of high expectation and high performance. With the facilities and coaching on offer, absolutely anything seemed possible. We knew that if either of our children showed extraordinary talent, they would be encouraged to develop it further. It was a huge move for us all, and so far it's been very worthwhile. It was a massive sacrifice for my husband and me, as life now revolves around the boys, particularly my son's cricket. In the first year since the move, I have already driven 25,000 miles. The majority of these were sport related. My son is now in his fourth year of playing for and representing his county. His dreams are growing, as is his love for the game and the cricketing environment. The discipline of sport is instilled in him, from the 7am training sessions, to the 350 hours of summer matches and the constant striving to improve. He takes nothing for granted and he knows only the best will be selected. Throughout this process, he's gained many life skills. The resilience, determination and discipline he has acquired are transferable to all aspects of life. We always say the basics are:

- ✓ Be memorable for the right reason
- ✓ Always look at and listen to the coach
- ✓ Take training seriously but also enjoy it
- ✓ Be confident
- ✓ Don't boast
- ✓ Say thank you at the end of each session

After all, everyone likes a coachable, polite child!

We feel it is our role as parents to research and facilitate the opportunities for our kids to excel in whatever they have shown an interest in. If this had been music, we would have done our research to the same level and facilitated opportunities in that field, moving schools accordingly. When the alarm goes off at 5:45am to get up for winter training, our boy never says he doesn't want to go. The day we have to push our children into their path is the day it is no longer their path. They lead – they have to. I have always done the research regarding where there are opportunities to play and train, but the choice is always with the boys. This even applies to our five year old, who is a developing tennis player and cricketer. He thinks it's normal to wake at 5:45am to train, and he plays tennis before school most days.

If you were to ask my son what he wants to do in life, he would reply, "Be a cricketer" and add that this will hopefully be for England. He is desperate for T20 Olympic cricket for 2024. As several Olympians have come from his school, he is very excited about the prospect of being an Olympic cricketer. I will never cap a desire, but he does also say he will be a banker as a backup! He is a strong mathematician, which I am sure is partly to do with his enjoyment of cricket, as it also engages his brain in this way, as he works out averages.

CHAPTER 30 - THE SECRET PARENTS: TRIALS AND TRIBULATIONS

As a family, we will all support him in chasing his cricket dream. Why not? He has truly found what he loves to do. We are acutely aware that the higher he is able to get, the further he will have to fall, but he does not let fear hold him back or weaken his passion and desire.

Being a 'sport parent' is not all fun and dreams. The day-to-day reality is far from glamorous. It involves long days, rushing to fit in homework, no 'play time', a lot of admin and even more washing – and then there are the other parents; the ones who want your child to lose so their own will look better. This is the hardest thing. Keeping calm and staying supportive is a must.

We have missed many parties and events and hardly manage to keep in touch with friends, as there is always a match miles away that we have to be at or get up early for. Summer is given over to cricket and that is how life is and will continue to be for many more years, especially seeing the talent in our five year old, who is following in his older brother's footsteps. The family has to be totally and utterly supportive and facilitate these opportunities. We also have to work out how county and regional systems work, both in what is said and those unsaid rules. Locating extra opportunities to be seen by the right people is part of our responsibility as parents. We want to guide our sons to be memorable for the right reasons, to be polite and to always listen to and thank the coaches. Above all, we want them to be coachable.

I don't believe talent alone will allow children to flourish. Not only is there the considerable financial investment to contemplate, but the personal sacrifice parents make in terms of time and energy makes it nothing short of an emotional rollercoaster. I see talented children whose parents have no intention of encouraging sport outside school hours or driving across the country, as it is inconvenient for them. It takes a whole family to commit. I have friends who cannot understand why we do what we do and say that we are mad. They ask, "What sort of childhood is this?" Well, my answer is, "A childhood that is delivering the most amazing opportunities to discover and learn so many of life's key lessons: resilience, teamwork, effective communication and discipline – the list goes on."

I'm just grateful that my son has found something that makes him happy. However, it hasn't all been roses. The stuff that has pissed me off is as follows:

- A Russian tennis player's parents refused to let their eight-year-old daughter compete for a 3/4th play-off place, as she could no longer win. Instead, she was dramatically marched off court with her father screaming at her. This also prevented another player from getting a rating.
- Independent schools regularly prioritise the selection of famous people's children in teams in order to please them (and possibly secure financial donations).
- I have seen parents in tears and throw tantrums around the coaches when their kids are not selected for teams.
- As petty as this may sound, after an exhausting season, I still get irritated by the kids who go for county trials and are told, in no uncertain terms, not to wear their own county attire so that it's an even field for everyone trying out. Yet the same kids always wear it to try and get that extra advantage. Follow the rules I say by wearing normal cricket gear and letting the talent speak for itself!

The greatest gift that sport has delivered to our family is that my son has found a sense of belonging in the world. Bring on the next match!

CHAPTER 31

The Wrong Type of Love and Parent Envy: How to Hinder Your Children

"Your child's success or lack of success in a certain sport does not determine what kind of parent you are." – Unknown

We have all seen it happen. Crazy parents on the side of the pitch, egos taking over, the doctor Steve Peters' chimp going into overdrive, and their emotional nonsense destroying the enjoyment of Sunday morning for all spectators. The craving to win is so high that the emotions and self-awareness of the parents becomes insufficient, which therefore hinders everyone who comes near them. These are the types of parents, who, according to them, have played a 'good game' in their time. These unconsciously incompetent people in our society are poison to youth development. Having children is a gift, but to then choose to live out their own failure through their offspring's sporting journey is criminal – yet it still happens so often. It is so wrong, oh so wrong. These louts are why it is so hard to enjoy football at youth level, and why many of my friends say they will encourage their kids to play rugby instead so that they will be around a different culture growing up. Who can blame them?

What's even more bizarre is that with so much campaigning in the media around how parents need to behave, many are still acting like ignorant fools. I do not doubt that they love their children, but it is the wrong type of love. Love without education causes issues for young athletes across the world in all sports. Being desperate for your child to win at any cost is truly wrong. We all want to win, of course. Life is about winning and losing, so I do not have an issue with young people learning that early on in their lives. But I worry about when this goes too far and when proving themselves by winning comes ahead of improving and getting better over the long term.

Pushy behaviour from parents has been proven to increase young athletes' stress levels. Can someone please tell me the point of winning 20-0 in a match week after week? I hear it and see it on social media all the time. Seriously, can someone tell me what the winning team will learn? What genuine challenges will they face? What areas of performance will they improve?

And then coupled with this there is the debate about dignity and respect for the opposition coaches. Come on everyone, think about it, and then behave in a way that shows class and mutual respect. Put the arrogance in the bin will you. Maybe coaches could use the following interventions:

- ✓ Offer to play fewer players.
- ✓ Rotate the team formation and positions.
- ✓ Get their own team to play with fewer touches.

I know that the better coaches do the above, but if I had my way after 5-0, I would make this compulsory across the country. I wonder if these idiot parents know the damage they could be doing by acting and interacting in the way they do. Often they are:

- ▸ Embarrassing their children.
- ▸ Making their children, and their friends, feel anxious about how they will behave on any given Sunday.
- ▸ Making their children feel edgy about their own performance in an environment that is meant to be safe and fun. As I call it, these children suffer from a pain in the brain.

Then there are the jealous parents, who envy the success of their children's friends. They show their true colours by failing to appreciate the accolades of others. This sends the wrong message to their children and promotes a jealous mentality amongst the rest of the team.

So, what can parents do to ensure they maximise their children's experiences of sport?

CHAPTER 31 - THE WRONG TYPE OF LOVE AND PARENT ENVY: HOW TO HINDER YOUR CHILDREN

> *Research has shown that positive parental involvement at grass roots level equates to greater enjoyment for all involved. At elite level, parents who display a supportive and caring nature, without judgment, are more likely to see their children reach professional level.*

The ones that do not get over involved are said to be the most effective. On the other hand, parents that unrealistically boost their children's egos and provide the wrong coaching advice often hinder progress the most. So, in summary, what type of parent are you? I'll let you decide.

SECTION SIX
Extra Time – The Extras…

This section of eight chapters relates to the random and quirky nature of life, football, people and society. It examines: the resilience that professional players require, the story of a former pro and the happiness he gained when released from the game, sports science in the elite environment and the importance of wellbeing and emotional intelligence. I also look at the theory of luck in football, along with the decreasing nature of effective dialogue in society.

CHAPTER 32

The Secret Footballer: Life After Football

"If I play football with my friends back in France, I can love football, but in England I knew nobody and I didn't speak English. Why did I come here? For a job. A career is only 10, 15 years. It's only a job. Yes, it's a good, good job and I don't say that I hate football, but it's not my passion." – Benoît Assou-Ekotto

This is the story of a former professional football player, who has been more satisfied with his life since he left the beautiful game.

As far back as I can remember, football has been my life. As a kid, if something wasn't football related then for the majority of the time I wasn't involved in it. I was lucky in that I showed talent from a young age, which resulted in me being at a professional club at the age of nine. At the time, this didn't mean a lot to me, as it was just another place to go and enjoy football. I was able to travel all over the country while my school friends played down the park. Year by year, the boys in my team would be whittled away and replaced, which was a strange experience, but I didn't know any different. I did notice, however, that as time progressed and I became slightly older, the environment gradually became more pressurised and, although enjoyment was still a key factor, it was clear that if you did not reach a certain level you were unlikely to still be there a year later. It was ruthless.

I was still at the club at 15, and I remember this was the time when all my focus had to go on gaining a full-time scholarship for the ages of 16 to 18. This was my chance to leave school and pursue the 'glory career', which I'd already put years of practice into. Although it was my choice whether to sign and accept the scholarship, there was no real choice involved. It was drilled into us that this is what we had worked hard for, so it would be ridiculous to turn it down – it was something to be proud of.

After beginning my scholarship, the transition from school to training full-time and playing every day was huge. Only one of my fellow players had started with me at the age of nine. So many boys came and went. On top of this emotion, I felt a million miles away from everyone I'd grown up with, but I was told many times that this sacrifice was worth it for the opportunity I'd been given. Looking back, I had convinced myself that this was my dream. However, I quickly learnt that the psychological side of the game was as big a challenge as the physical one. This is something that young players are rarely warned about. At times, I would question whether this was what I wanted in my life, but I quickly brushed this thought aside by reminding myself of the 'fortunate' position I was in. I was proud to be where I was, and my full focus had to go on getting to the next step – a professional contract and my name and squad number on the back of my shirt.

It was unheard of for someone not to pursue this dream, or so I thought. I remember that for months on end I would leave my house in the dark and return in the dark exhausted. I was earning little money, but again this was all in aid of reaching the goal that for more than nine years I had worked so hard for. It was a strange environment to be in at that age, and I'd guess it's one that is unique to football. At times, I felt you had to have a certain personality to fit into the culture. On occasions it could be brutal.

So, after two years of hard work and sacrifice, I was offered a professional contract, which is easily one of the biggest achievements of my life. It meant that I would no longer see the majority of the teammates and friends I'd spent every day of the last two years with, but that was part and parcel of it; something I had been experiencing since I was a kid. I suppose it was the survival of the fittest. I'd now reached the biggest stage, and one that promised to bring so much.

My first year as a professional flew by and wasn't what I expected at all. I felt in a strange no man's land between the scholarship and the dream of first-team football. On one hand, I was living the life that I'd dreamt about; on the other, it all went too quickly. Day after day of hard work and mental strain passed, but I still questioned whether I had any chance at all, as I was frozen out almost immediately after I arrived. I found myself

CHAPTER 32 - THE SECRET FOOTBALLER: LIFE AFTER FOOTBALL

sacrificing enjoyment for the cause. It felt like I'd jumped onto a conveyor belt to be launched forward a year, by which time I'd either be chucked off or moved onto the next one. I was only 19 and didn't have a lot to show for it but memories. I spent the year working hard but never felt like I was involved in what was going on around me. It was a year full of highs and lows, which ended abruptly. I was simply sent into an office and told I was no longer required. I couldn't help but think that the big opportunity was actually a very small one. For the first time I had to question who I was without football as my guide. What I found bizarre is that the support I received around player care to get to professional level vanished when I became one. I had no one to share my thoughts with or go over what could be improved. After 10 years it was all over.

After my release, I had to learn about the real world outside the football bubble I lived in – and pretty damn quick. Luckily enough, I overcame the initial devastation and focused on different interests, some of which I never knew I had. Since then, I have been told by close family members and friends that I am twice the person I was when I was a professional football player, and I have grown and changed for the better. Although I cannot help but regret leaving the life I so wanted, I can now look back on it fondly having learnt from it all. The positives are that now I have other focuses in my life, I feel a sense of freedom, and I have learnt a lot about myself in the process. Perhaps if I had been more open-minded during my time at the club, I would have been more prepared, but the environment was not one in which I felt able to openly consider anything else other than what was going on there and then.

I am proud and thankful for being able to experience it, and strangely grateful for the positive change it forced me to make in my life moving forwards. Onto the next chapter, as they say. I was playing semi-professional football, but these days I'm not even doing that. I need some time out from the game I loved. I have a coaching job and I'm happier than I have ever been. Football was a huge part of my life, but it's not everything, as I have grown to learn. They often say the grass is never greener, but I believe it actually is.

CHAPTER 33

The Story of True Resilience: Our Journey

by Ebere Eze

"Tough times never last, but tough people do." – Robert Schuller

My first encounter with Steve Sallis was in 2008, I was 11 years old and it was at one of my year-seven school football matches. He was the manager of the other team. Yes, you heard it right, the opposition's teacher! I attended John Roan School based in Greenwich, South East London, and Steve was the PE teacher at Blackheath Bluecoat School, our nearest local rivals, which Rio and Anton Ferdinand once attended. One of the reasons why Steve has been a lasting mentor for me is because of how he went about coaching his team. Although we had played against Blackheath Bluecoat in many league and cup games, that day was a friendly fixture.

His Bluecoat team were equal to us, but both of the teams were performing poorly. Goals were flying in left, right and centre and the passing quality was appalling. There were lots of long balls and ugly football being played. You could see the frustration in Steve's eyes – and hear it too. Now, a normal teacher would have waited until half time to talk to his team and re-gather their tactics, but not Steve. I remember him walking onto the pitch during the first half and saying, "Stop! Everyone sit down where you are." I laughed with my fellow schoolmates out of complete confusion. "What is this crazy man doing telling us what to do?" we said to each other. "He's not our coach, he's theirs!"

He then started to talk to everyone about how to play football as a team and how to work together to win, by passing better, receiving on the half turn and making space by not doing it all alone. At the time, as an academy player at Arsenal, I thought it was a moment of madness, of course. Who is this guy telling us what to do? But as I have grown up and matured I've realised that the way Steve went about things that day is the reason why he remains one of my mentors today. He simply wants to get the best out of everyone around him. Steve sees the bigger picture, like he did on that day. He is unique, very smart and selfless, and that's why I have kept close to Steve. He has my back, and I have his.

My Story

My footballing career started off at eight, at a local side called Bruin FC, which was based in Thamesmead, about 15-minutes east from where I was brought up in Greenwich. I was there for about a season and a half before professional clubs started to show an interest in the majority of that Bruin side, including myself. Of all the clubs that were willing to sign me, choosing Arsenal was a pretty easy choice because of how much of a huge fan I was. I was there for five years (until the end of U13s) before they released me. This was heartbreaking, as Arsenal was all that I knew at this time and it had never crossed my mind that I may not ever play for them. Despite this setback, I knew I had to keep going, which led to me signing for Fulham Football Club after a short trial. I'd yet to fully recover from the mental turmoil of being released by Arsenal. I remember facing them a year after my release and tears welling up as I played them.

After an up and down three years with Fulham, I was then released for the second time in my career, in the middle of the U16s season. Of course, being released is never a nice thing, but I believe it was a lot easier for me this time, due to the fact that I was not completely happy with football and life. The main emotion I went through was not anger at being released by Fulham, it was more the fear of not having a club. I'd also moved schools in order to go to Fulham. It was so close to the scholarship season, which, as a youth footballer, is the be all and end all. Fortunately, a friend who had also left Fulham was now at Reading Football Club and he pushed them to have a look at me. After two training sessions and a game against the U18s, Reading seemed keen on signing me to the end of the season, whilst they decided whether I was worthy of a two-year scholarship. Even though the club had expressed interest in me, my confidence levels were still extremely low, which inevitably affected my performance. This eventually started to show and resulted in me being released yet again, for the third time, at the end of the season.

At this point, I didn't even have enough time to be upset about Reading. The only thing going through my mind was panic, as the scholarships had already been given out. I've had a club all my life, so this was a completely new experience for my family and me. I remember praying and crying myself to sleep at night because I couldn't see any light at the end of the tunnel.

Thankfully, one of my old coaches at Fulham, Dan Thomas, called me with some great news. He told me that Millwall Football Club would have me in from the start of pre-season. The month of off-season that had come to feel like a year had finally ended and my trial had started. I did two weeks of training and played a couple of matches before the decision was made to give me a scholarship. Wow, the relief of finally being at a club again was immense, and I thanked God for it. I could finally start enjoying my football again, which is what I did for the first year of my time at Millwall, where I was reunited with Steve, who was now working there with the U18s. I hoped that my second year at the club would be as good as my first. However, things did not work out the way I would have liked and after another season of ups and downs, I was then released for the fourth time in my career. It was a tough time and I was back to what I felt was square one. I panicked about whether to apply for university or not. My agent was confident throughout this period that I would find the club that was best suited to me, and rightly so. After a few more trials and a couple of rejections, Queens Park Rangers, my fifth club, offered me my first professional contract. Words cannot describe the feeling. Even today, I thank God for seeing me through that difficult time, and for allowing me to find my more confident self at QPR. I now play regularly in the first team and have recently represented England at U20 level.

Advice

To all the young people out there playing football, my advice to you is to never give up. No matter how hard things may seem, it is important to believe in yourself, especially when nobody else does. You need to have faith that there is light at the end of the tunnel. It might be hard to believe this at the time of your distress, but the more you believe and the more confidence you have in yourself, the more certain you are to achieve success.

Today

I often get caught up in wanting to do better and be better, which is good, but I do not spend enough time appreciating how far I have come within the last year, let alone my career so far. I am now buzzing when I go into training every day and I am finally enjoying my football, which in the end is the most important thing. I thank God for all that he has blessed me with, including a handful of amazing coaches, managers and members of staff that I have met along the way, namely Steve for keeping me sane through a lot of hard times and for reassuring me that I can be as big and successful as I want to be – if I put my mind to it. I would finally like to thank my family and friends for sticking by me and for providing the most amazing support system.

Ebs x

CHAPTER 34

"Sports Science Appliance"

My Experiences of Sport Scientists in Football

"He ate ice cream for breakfast, drank beer for lunch ... But as a player? Oh, beautiful, beautiful. I loved that boy." – The former Lazio manager, Dino Zoff, on his admiration for Paul Gascoigne.

I'll admit that, in general, I am not terribly knowledgeable about this topic. Even when I studied A Level PE, it was always my weakest subject. I regard myself as a social scientist and not a sport scientist. My peers laugh, as I always like to ask questions related to sport science, which at least enables me to have basic knowledge. The Millwall physio staff members who need thanking for putting up with me and my profligacy over these matters back then are: Nick Irwin, Adam Johnson, Steve Brown, Mick Mcduff and Jonjo Hurley. All were proper blokes and they are still mates to this day. They are another example of the great institution that is Millwall Football Club. Proper people!

Like any life-long learner, I am constantly looking to collaborate and improve myself by stealing knowledge from my peers about this process, in particular, for elite performers. Training load, minutes played, rehab and prehab are all areas that need expertise at the top level. Twenty years ago, whilst at university in London, I actually studied with about 300 sport science students. I chose to be a Physical Education teacher simply because I didn't love sport science enough to choose it as a career, and I was rubbish at it.

Whilst at university, I lived and played football with a highly successful strength and conditioning coach called Karl Halabi. He has worked under

Brendan Rodgers, with Paul Clement at Swansea City, and also at clubs such as Chelsea, Fulham, Reading, Watford and Derby.

Now, why has Karl been a sustained success?

Firstly, he was dedicated to his subject area; secondly, he was the first of my university cohorts to do a Masters degree back in the late '90s. Finally, Karl was a former youth player at Reading, so knew his football inside and out. He was a quality full back in his day and had the attributes of many professional players. These experiences made him the perfect role model and enabled him to fulfil his potential for many years to come.

Sport scientists, strength and conditioning coaches and physios are an interesting breed, though. In my experience, and just like in any industry, some are good and some are bad. However, my biggest observation about strength and conditioning coaches in general is that many are too often 'zooming in' rather than 'zooming out'.

What do I mean?

I mean the bigger picture. Often they are very outcome focused and do not always look at the broader picture regarding WHAT holistic development is and what the journey feels and looks like for their athletes.

What do I mean by *outcome focused*?

From my experience, some conditioning coaches simply think that a gym programme, a six-week testing cycle, a little or a lot of data and football training alone is going to bring natural gains for players. Well, it is, of course, but my question to them is this:

> *Are you maximising this experience to capitalise on the learning potential for the athletes?*

My advice is vast, but my main message is for them to try and think like teachers, and have a mindset that they are not a coach, because in my eyes they are the former. In my experience, teachers and coaches can often be miles apart, and they employ different methods. It is well known that historically, a teaching methodology is much deeper and has more meat on the bone. Coaching can sometimes be superficial and lacking in substance. This ineffective style is confirmed by research from Bloom's taxonomy, which refers to basic learning as 'rote learning'. (Bloom's taxonomy was created in 1956 under the leadership of educational psychologist Dr Benjamin Bloom, in order to promote higher forms of thinking in education rather than just remembering facts – rote learning. It is most often used when designing educational, training and learning processes.)

In summary, here's my advice for sports scientists and strength and conditioning coaches:

1. Be a teacher of the subject rather than coaching it. Facilitate knowledge in order to make the subject of sport science come alive for athletes. Be someone who flips it and makes the athletes believe they should complete their prehab, rehab and weights programme because it's the right thing to do – rather than something that they have just been told to do. Tell stories of horror and tales of joy to inspire young and old aspiring footballers. Basically, get that personality out!

2. Try to understand people and the learning process better. Utilise the expertise around you and ask staff for techniques, hints and tips about how you can improve the actual teaching element of what you know. In other words, don't do the testing or weights programmes where players are made to wait in a long line like you would at a bus stop. I call them 'bus queues'. That teaching and coaching strategy really is Mickey Mouse delivery. If you're going to incorporate fun activities with players, such as races and drills, that's great, but why have three teams of five when you can have five teams of three? This would result in more movement, more fun and more gains for players physically, psychologically and socially. Stop looking inwards (zooming in) and start to look outwards.

3. Eliminate boredom at all costs. This is my point about some strength and conditioning coaches. You're a TEACHER, and not

just an outcome-based practitioner. Your role with the athletes is far bigger and greater than that! Inspire them, laugh with them, laugh at them, laugh at yourself. It all helps you to help them.

4. Bring the data you use back to life. Training and testing is for a reason, and not just from the fabric of a spreadsheet or laptop! Stop talking to them about squatting, etc., and teach them how and why they squat. Bring the data off the page and explain what it means and how it relates to being a footballer throughout every moment of every day. In education, we call this contextualised learning, i.e. what does this leg exercise, training methodology and strategy mean to me on training or match day? In terms of data and assessment, it's called AFL, which means Assessment for Learning. FYI, this is the number one trick of the trade!

5. Make your words create pictures! Richard Akenhead, with whom I worked at England, was a superb practitioner and great at doing this with the players. He would tell stories and use metaphors to teach these under-15 players about their bodies and how they were equivalent to a supercar. When describing sprinting, turning and decelerating, he would say that supercars not only have the best engines, oil and petrol and drive the fastest, they also have the best brakes and slow down the quickest in order to change direction. You could see the kids' faces light up at the description. To be fair, I was the same! The kids truly understood what he meant, as did I. On the story of effective language, another high-quality youth coach is Harry Watling of West Ham United. His use of words to describe and explain content for young athletes is the best I have ever seen. I call him a 'wizard with words'. He is always creating pictures with words and his use of vocabulary is superb. Harry will succeed in the coaching industry, so watch this space. He's a true professional and, most importantly, a gentleman of the great game.

Back to sport science now. Over the years, I have asked professional players these questions about the appliance of sport science:

CHAPTER 34 - "SPORTS SCIENCE APPLIANCE"

- Do you know why you are doing that exercise? The answer, sadly, is often the same: "No, not really."

- Do you know what your test score is for your 30m sprint or single leg squat? Unbelievably, they say no again. I mean, WOW! In terms of elite education, those players should be absolutely crystal clear about all of their data. It should be tattooed and emblazoned on their forehead. This data should be talked about, used, discussed, shared, challenged, questioned and, above all, understood like it's the Bible. Otherwise, why do it?

This is another of my points regarding academy football in particular. Strength and conditioning coaches might know a lot about scientific material, but in order to have the greatest impact on the athletes they support, they *need to know and understand about 'learning' and how the human brain operates*. This is what I mean by 'outcome based'. Some of the methods I have witnessed are failing the athletes and, therefore, are flawed. Now, I am not talking about teaching the squatting technique or the single leg lunge, I'm talking about the importance of bringing to life everything you do as a teacher of the subject. This could include using learning to learn techniques (also known as meta-learning), video analysis, video diaries of previous players, podcasts, interviews and SurveyMonkey, etc. The best strength and conditioning teachers and physios I have worked with have similar traits. They ask question after question in order to create the best learning environment for the players. They seek to improve their understanding of what teaching and learning really is, and what it looks and feels like for them and their athletes. Their emotional intelligence is far greater, and this is why Paul Stretch, in particular, stood out. If any sport science lecturers are reading this, my advice is that you need to implement teaching and learning in your university programme ASAP. Because if you don't, all you are doing is failing the future prospects and potential of the strength and conditioning coaches out there.

Now, before all you sport science coaches begin to think I am bashing you, let me promise you that I am not. Many close relationships I've had in my working career have been with sport science coaches, and I've seen them doing great work. But my advice is to start zooming out and think of your role on a greater scale. The guys that have had to put up with working with me, Paul Stretch in particular (who will be a close friend for life), but also Ian Jones, Alex Berger and Darren Stern, are all top-class professionals. Most importantly, they are top-class people. These are men that the players respected greatly and who deserve a mention.

CHAPTER 35

The Theory of Luck in Football!

And How You Need It! A Professional and Semi-Professional Perspective

"I didn't see, but the people tell me it was offside. You need some luck to win the game. Always in football, sometimes it is for you, sometimes it is against you." – Mauricio Pochettino

There is nothing more annoying than when people say that you make your own luck. If that were the case, no one would win the lottery, would they? I have been buying tickets every week, twice a week, since 1994 and have won just £10 in all that time. Last year, however, I watched my television screen closely. It was the 2017 UEFA Champions League quarter final and Real Madrid clearly got lucky versus Bayern Munich in the game. Decision after decision went against Munich, and it was for all to see. The refereeing incompetence simply cost them and Madrid went on to win in that tie with bundles of luck.

Gary Player, the famous golfer, once said: "The harder you work the luckier you get."

But is this really true? Having been involved in non-league football at the coal face for 10 years in management, as well as professional football, I can really see how luck plays an integral part in success in sport. My former colleague at Millwall, Larry McAvoy, who was the U18s coach, regularly used to laugh to me on a Monday over a coffee about how much 'luck' had been present in the weekend's professional games. We would chuckle about how much good fortune was linked to certain goals, and how this would correlate with actual results more often than not. After all, poor results cost people their jobs. So when I mean luck, I do not mean the stuff you and your team are in control of, I'm trying to explain the things that happen in sport that are out of your control, such as:

- Referee competence or incompetence.
- Opposition's talent – or lack of talent on any given day.
- Fixture list congestion.

On balance, I do not think anyone can argue about the many variables that go on in any given sport that make or break results on any given day. Sport is about fine margins and football is no different. But most importantly, we need to remember that the element of luck going either way can affect people's jobs and careers. If we look at the 1966 World Cup final, there is still debate to this day about Geoff Hurst's second goal. Looking at it objectively, I believe it did not cross the line, and if the decision went against us, it could have changed the history of our country forever.

The season I remember the most is the 2016-17 one at Leatherhead FC. We had many moments of what you could say were a variation of luck, bad luck and things that were certainly out of any manager's control. We played Canvey Island at home in late January and, without exaggeration, could have been 5-0 down at half time, as their centre forward missed chance after chance. We went in losing 1-0 and thanking our lucky stars. The game ended with a 1-1 score and I do not care what anyone says – we got lucky.

One month later, we played AFC Sudbury at home and were cruising at 1-0 up when in reality it should have been 3-0 to us. But we all know what a 1-0 score line is like, as until your team gets the second goal it is never over in football. In the 70th minute, Sudbury's forward went through clear on goal, when our centre half got the wrong side to defend him properly and literally hauled him down in what looked like a rugby tackle. It was a blatant straight red card for our player. The whole ground was waiting to see the appropriate card, but the referee failed to produce it. How, I will never know. Jimmy and I were in stitches. The ref's incompetent decision went in our favour. In my world, that is lucky. Consequently, Sudbury and Canvey got relegated that season. Was that the single and only reason for

CHAPTER 35 - THE THEORY OF LUCK IN FOOTBALL!

their relegation? Of course not, but that lack of luck didn't help either of them.

In the penultimate match of the season, we played the Metropolitan Police away, which we won 1-0. Our goal was a high-quality set piece. Our opponents then bombarded us for the entire second half with long balls into our penalty area. Their centre half somehow missed three clear headers from six yards out, and I haven't even talked about the luck part yet! This came when their centre forward got fouled inside the area. It was obvious that this should have led to a penalty against us, but on this day somehow, the referee in question did not award a foul, as had happened in the Sudbury game. Jim Cooper, the opposing manager, was understandably upset, and who wouldn't be? I would have been the same. It was a truly shocking refereeing decision, which again I regard as luck. These moments are easy to forget in victory. But I choose to see the facts. It is a shame that many people in football are very blinkered about these moments.

I could, of course, make a list treble the size about the decisions and moments that did not go our way that season, including the time Jimmy and I both got sent to the stands in the same game, but in actual fact I was a naughty school boy and hid in the dug-out behind our player Giuseppe Sole for the last 30 minutes as the ref had lost complete control – a funny moment where I admit I twisted the rules. Not my best life decision. I will mention another trend around luck, however. During one of the mid-season months, we had a string of six games where we missed guilt-edged chances to score and win every game by two or three goals. We ended up winning only one and lost all the other five games by a single goal. Who does the blame lie with? The manager? The players? Or is it the fault of the referees?

On these occasions, the blame lay with all of the above. So, is it unlucky that your centre forward misses all these chances, even after hours of practice, or that your goalkeeper makes needless errors? I will let you decide, but the variables of sport are so vast that who knows? In my experience, many non-league footballers blame everyone else but themselves. I call them fake (and most people in the know are aware that the game is full of fakes).

These people are often too weak and too stupid to look at themselves. Instead they possess only one skill, and that is to blame others.

It's said that luck evens out over a season, but I am not always sure. Maybe it does over a lifetime. In summary, the standard of refereeing during that season in the Isthmian Premier was nothing short of poor. There are some excellent referees and linesmen at all different levels, of course, and win or lose I have expressed this to them, which I think is important for them to hear. It is not rocket science to attempt to explain decisions to players, but so many still fail to do so. I think it's sad for them and sad for the game of football. I have always believed, and always will, that players make thousands more errors than referees in any sport, but while many of the younger referees may have knowledge of the rules, they are sadly devoid of any social savvy. What's even more infuriating is that some are not even fit enough to keep up with play, and some do not want to. This is so much the case that Jimmy and I genuinely reckoned at one time that we were fitter than some of them. In one match, against Kingstonian at home, the referee, who was about 18-stone, genuinely failed to leave the centre circle for the entire 90 minutes. That really is Sunday pub league stuff. I expect that from older officials and a lower level of the game, but not referees in their 20s and 30s! My final gripe is that referees have yet to work out that, as in any sport, the more skilful players get fouled more than the less skilful ones, therefore there will undoubtedly be more fouls given for the better teams. I thought everyone knew that.

I've written this chapter because I applaud all the managers and head coaches who have devoted their lives to their respective sports and have been doing so for many years. I salute you! What a tough profession. I say the same for those at amateur level, who are doing all this on top of their day jobs.

Luck for the Professional Player

People that truly know the game of football will know that as much as the vast majority of professional players have worked hard to become the successes they are, there are many elements, such as grit, passion and high

CHAPTER 35 - THE THEORY OF LUCK IN FOOTBALL!

levels of skill that have got them there. In contrast, there are many athletes floating about outside of the professional game who possess equal quality and dedication, but just did not get the breaks they needed. The variables of someone's sporting life and journey are vast. I thought I knew the game well before I was involved at professional level, but until you live it, it is impossible to truly get to grips with the luck that happens at elite level. In terms of the 16-18 professional scholarship programme, the first and second year squad has to consist of roughly 20 players that fill all of the positions on the pitch. So players in one particular position sometimes have an advantage of being signed compared to others, over any given season, depending on who is in the age group above and who is below. Basically at this level, the selection process works on a two-year cycle. This means that timing is everything.

I always relate elite football to the film *Sliding Doors*. At times, the game really is luck-fuelled. People outside the industry also assume that because the premier league players earn so much money, every professional club must have bundles of cash and can therefore sign as many good players as they feel necessary. However, this simply is not case, as many clubs are failing businesses. As an example, players who live far away from the location of the club won't be signed because the club cannot afford to pay for their accommodation. It's crazy but true.

It's not uncommon for a player to gain a scholarship over another player simply because they live nearer to the club. They often don't possess more ability, but they save the club thousands of pounds a year in accommodation alone. This is the side to the game that people don't know about, and therefore I regard it as another lucky element to athletes' careers.

> As the saying goes, "It's not what you know, but who you know." This also stands firm in sporting circles. It's incredible how many doors get opened for certain players over other ones.

Using players who are in the process of going for trials as an example, their success depends on so many variables:

- Whether a certain agent has better contacts in one club compared to another, etc.
- The injury factor. A regular scenario is a player getting injured, which then spells a chance of success for someone else. For example, the player below them in the pecking order gets a one-off chance in the first team, which is down to luck rather than skill and application. As an athlete you have no control over this, other than to be ready for the chance when it comes.

I have always said that for every defending left back in football, there are five right backs as good as the left-footed player. 'Leftys' are sought after and rare in the game, and they give a team needed balance. Let me emphasise that left-footed players like Messi and Maradona were not lucky, but you get my point I hope. Luck really is needed to be successful in professional sport, but it's what you do with it when you get it that counts. My final point about luck is the coach and academy manager you get. Leaders that deal with facts and not opinions and emotions are a God send. The type of bosses who live off their opinions make and certainly break careers!

CHAPTER 36

Insecure PERSON multiplied by Incompetent PERSON
=
DANGEROUS PERSON

"Arrogance, ignorance and incompetence. Not a pretty cocktail of personality traits in the best of situations. No sirree. Not a pretty cocktail in an office-mate and not a pretty cocktail in a head of state. In fact, in a leader, it's a lethal cocktail." – Graydon Carter

Let's be honest, in football and life there are dodgy people. We've all met them.

- The backstabbers in the workplace.
- The types of people who have nothing better to say than negative things about you or other people.
- The people that spend their life covering their own backside.
- The sour footballers that are out of the team and thus create poison in the dressing room.

Why do these people act in this way?

As my mum used to say, "Unless you've got something positive to say about someone, don't say it at all." That is really worth thinking about!

So, what about these people mentioned above? Let's start with the following quote:

"Confidence is silent, insecurities are loud."

Insecure people and incompetence often go hand in hand in society, and very much within a football changing room full of adults. From my experience, insecure people are often this way because they are incompetent and therefore feel threatened. Get it? Incompetent people often fail in work and life, which makes them become more insecure, and so the negative cycle continues.

To put it bluntly, these people are potentially dangerous and they exist all over football and professional industries. They usually have nothing else to worry and think about apart from other people's lives. Staying on the football topic, players and many staff display traits such as the following.

They:

- Blame others and never admit wrongdoings
- Lack trust in themselves and others
- Get satisfaction from the failures of others, instead of trying to bail them out
- Have self-serving agendas
- Display general inefficiency
- Fail to honour commitments

Thinking outside of football, when a workplace has several of these people it means that there is a real problem within the dynamics. There is a saying that I learnt from my teaching days many years ago. It goes, "Like hangs around with like."

Football clubs are no different. So often these people attract each other: the good to the good and the bad to the bad. *The law of attraction* is something I believe in massively. I have talked about the unconscious incompetence of people who are not aware of their behaviours at all, but sometimes people know exactly what they are doing to upset the process for all. These consciously incompetent folk are therefore aware of their negative behaviours. I am not really sure which is worse, knowing that you are not a genuinely good person or not having a clue that you aren't one.

CHAPTER 36 - INSECURE PERSON MULTIPLIED BY INCOMPETENT PERSON = DANGEROUS PERSON

I do know, however, that these blaggers are worth avoiding, and I advise you to pick your colleagues wisely and ensure you work alongside the conscientious folk. I have been pretty fortunate in my career and have worked with loads of skilled people. My cultural experiences in the workplace have been generally positive, but it hasn't always been that way. As with most experiences, and the varied people that we work with, I believe that genuine intelligence comes with certain behaviours, which correlate heavily to positivity. However, watch out for the: *Insecure x incompetent person (x = multiplied)*. Unless they have a growth mindset and want to improve and learn, they can be really *dangerous*. Sadly, most of these people wouldn't have a clue what a growth mindset is in the first place, and if they did they wouldn't understand how to change. These people are often fixed in thoughts, flippant with their emotions, stubborn with their ways, moody with their persona and spoilt when they do not get their way. They are unwilling to change, and that's even if they know they need to change in the first place!

Which type of person are you?

CHAPTER 37

"It's OK not to be OK"

Working with Young People – The Joys and the Pitfalls!

"I love working with children, and I have learned to be very patient with them." – Princess Diana

Player care in professional football is finally improving. I have to give credit to Spencer Hidge from the *Premier Sports Network*. This great company has driven clubs to understand that the duty of care for elite athletes needs enhancing on a national basis. League Football Education (LFE) and the Premier League education department are also transforming the game in a positive way. In modern-day football, player agents are vital cogs in the wheel, and I need to thank the many open-minded agents who have asked for my expertise where I continue to help their players.

Dealing with young people can be incredibly inspiring, yet it can also be crucifying. They give us joy, but often lead us to stress. I have found that many adults working in a professional environment, whether that is as a teacher or coach, often struggle to deal with their own emotions, let alone those of others, and thus cannot empathise with the people in front of them – adult or child. The best of the best educators, whether they are at a school, university or a professional football club, manage to listen, adjust and have a structured cognitive rationale and the mental toolbox to help the mindsets of the athletes they serve. I have often said that the coaches who can only shout at players are motivating no one but themselves. They simply do not know any other way, as they do not possess any other tools.

Now, I would be lying if I said I hadn't evolved myself over the past 20 years of coaching and teaching. By naturally reflecting on the good and the bad, I believe we become better at dealing with the various situations that occur with the people we support. Working with current, elite and aspiring professional athletes, I have seen first-hand the stress that some of these athletes are under. Their burdens can include: performance and peer pressure; school, family, relationship and financial worries; and addiction. I currently mentor many professional golfers who are so worried about their next pay cheque, because performance pressure prevents them from doing so. For younger athletes, exams can ramp up the pressure even further. In addition, what about dealing with bereavement at a young age, or serious illness, or many other life variables that come our way? Over the years, I have sadly witnessed many young people trying to deal with these life-changing experiences.

So, please remember that young people and athletes are often stressed, worried or fearful.

> So, my advice for all young athletes, parents and the educators that support them is to understand that it's OK not to be OK.

I once listened to a podcast with Frank Dick, the former Great Britain Athletics boss. He talked about being "comfortable with being uncomfortable". I thought this was a great example of how many athletes feel at any level. The advice is to almost accept that this is the case when competing or trying to accept life's ups and downs. The same idiom can be used about life, of course. I am aware that some UK schools have implemented a wellbeing and mental health curriculum. Sadly, these processes are not implemented enough in schools or in workplaces, which is something my business has made great strides in supporting.

The success picture featured on the next page is a great metaphor for what success really looks like versus what people think it looks like. In my experience, both the old and the young often think that success is easy to come by and is achieved based on ability and talent alone. As the experts, we all know that ability and talent simply is not enough for sustained success. My theory is that athletes may fluke it in the short-term, and may make a debut at professional level, but in the medium and long-term, talent alone will never be enough for the majority. Therefore, creating resilience and character development programmes is vital. In the past, I have introduced meta-learning programmes for athletes.

An example of this process is a language framework. When I was at Millwall Football Club, I created a glossary of terms (learning to learn document), where the language was agreed, which meant that players and staff alike could understand it. Educators, teachers and coaches often assume their players understand what they say, especially when they respond with a nod of their heads. In reality, students often haven't got a clue what the coach is talking about. This happens a lot even in adult football where players are too fearful to speak up in front of their peers when they don't understand something.

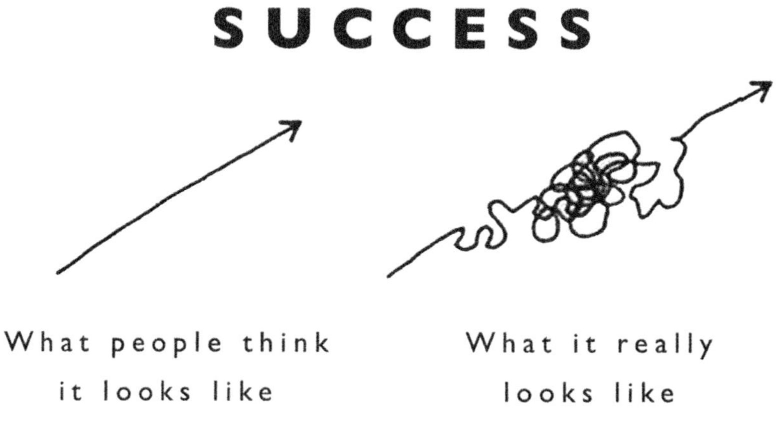

SUCCESS

What people think it looks like

What it really looks like

Figure 5: Success model

I felt that giving the players a repertoire and a bank of language, including speaking skills, self-assessment methodology and questioning techniques, was key in order for them to not just learn about football, but to learn about learning. Additionally, this meta-learning process would help them learn about being better at their game. Complicated, right? No, it's actually very simple. The learning to learn strategy included providing techniques for how to ask better questions. The players initially found this an interesting and demanding experience. Asking good questions is harder than you think, particularly considering the fear factor that athletes have when in front of their peers. They often see it as a sign of weakness. The glossary included a bank of questions for the players to try and use. This helped give a greater depth to their learning, and I would use this strategy by not always giving the obvious answers. One of the questions in the player's glossary included: *"What are the possible solutions to this problem I have (on or off the field)?"*

Basically, many young people often struggle to understand the 'off the field' part of life. Mental health issues are becoming more common in society; therefore, we as educators *need* to understand that young people sometimes don't understand life.

And if that makes sense to you, you may then understand how this becomes a cycle of mental torture for the athlete. Dealing with emotions is hard enough for adults, let alone young people. They may have peer pressure eating away at them, and they may find it hard to express themselves, even to the people they can trust. I know, as I have personally struggled with this in my past. But remember, always say to them that, *"Sometimes it's OK not to be OK."*

CHAPTER 38

The Death of Dialogue

"The more social media we have, the more we think we are connecting, yet in reality we are really disconnecting from each other." – JR (artist)

I'm watching Sky Sports on a match day. My TV screen zooms into the players' tunnel, as the superstar professionals get off the coach to walk into the dressing room. And nearly every single one of them has earphones on and a bloody hoodie. Good or bad? Now, let me tell you this. I have mentioned marginal gains loads of times in this book. Would you like another random one? Here goes…

Do not buy club tracksuits with hoods on! Why? Because it means players are even less likely to talk than they do already. Crazy but true – hoodies really piss me off.

I would also ban hoodies in schools, and I'd put a stop to Twitter, Facebook, Instagram, Snapchat and generally any of the internet tools that we communicate via in modern society. In the last 20 years, face-to-face interaction has disappeared at a rapid rate. Back in my day, and before the email revolution, if you wanted a job done in a school you would walk 10-minutes down the corridor and have a chat with your colleague. You would interact with them, hopefully build a relationship, and solve the problem via face-to-face contact.

Now?

You either send a text message, email or tweet someone. I am fond of social media and think it has a positive place in modern society, but I must admit I get more joy out of meeting my mate Gary Alexander for our customary weekly fry up in a South London café, playing golf with my dad, talking to Livers on the phone during our weekly Thursday night 'chatathon' (which can last hours) and meeting the Leatherhead lads for a catch up face to face. We know, of course, that relationships in life are a key component to our happiness. The assumption that money equates to happiness is important to think about. Can it really make us truly happy? If that were the case, premier league footballers and film stars would never suffer from mental illness. In my opinion, the reason why we live in this world is not because of money, but healthy relationships which give us positive energy. When people talk to me about making money from this book, I laugh. It is well known that books make you little money. I wrote this book because I want to help people like you.

We have WhatsApp groups for everything these days: work, departments within work, family, siblings and football or university friends. All of these have a place as far as modern communication is concerned. On balance, they help us stay in touch with people. However, I believe there is a danger of WhatsApp overkill – a bit like emails, I suppose. It baffles me when big businesses or people in work send the dreaded 'all staff email' but sadly about complete bullshit. I call these 'drainer emails', as they are basically a waste of everyone's time and do not improve the performance of the institution whatsoever. I have worked with many different personalities over many years who send these types of emails. In my experience, they are either, "Hi everyone, oooh, it's my birthday today, I have left cakes in the staffroom." Or, "Hi all, I've lost my red pen, has anyone seen it?" I am not against work colleagues celebrating birthdays of course, but I'm against people sending crap emails about birthdays while at the same time they haven't sent anything all year about how they are improving the business or team. These people add no value and waste people's time.

Young people worry me more and more. Year on year and generation upon generation, I notice that their communication skills are getting worse. Many of the following behaviours are portrayed regularly:

- Little eye contact.
- Not asking how you are.

CHAPTER 38 - THE DEATH OF DIALOGUE

- Conversations that last no more than 30 seconds and include regular grunts.
- Poor body language.

The amount of times I have asked a young person, "How are you today?" only to be met with the response, "Yep, fine." End of conversation it is then!

Most of the people I've worked with have no doubt seen me respond a thousand times to this noncommittal reply. I usually playfully mock them by pretending to ask myself how I am and how my day is going. I do this jokingly but purposefully, in order to educate the child about how they need to act in the future. I am sending the subliminal message that taking an interest in other people is important in life, and is a vital ingredient of great leaders.

To be fair, I need to thank my dad for this. Even as a four year old, I remember him saying to me: "Son, everyone you meet, look them in the eye, shake their hand, say hello and ask them how they are."

However, it's not always young people that communicate poorly, of course. What about those people you speak with on the phone who cut you off in order to speak to someone else? WTF is that all about? It's proper rude. And what about the meetings you have sat in, where people's mobile phones have been more of a hindrance than a help? The device sits there face up and kills the atmosphere and productivity every time it goes off. I believe this is another example of a complete lack of self-awareness. As Simon Sinek states, "Put the mobiles away and listen properly."

So, people:

- ✓ Start calling rather than texting all the time.
- ✓ Start walking and talking rather than emailing.
- ✓ Start meeting and greeting.
- ✓ Stop thinking of yourself and think of others.

And to all athletes:

- Put the earphones away and talk to your teammates. Find out about them. Listen to them. Learn about them. We all like music, but in my opinion this individual experience should be shared by everyone in the changing room.

CHAPTER 39

10 Tips for 'Emotional Intelligence' in Sport and Why it's Number One for SUCCESS!

"It is not the size of a man but the size of his heart that matters."
– Evander Holyfield

Emotional intelligence is a widely talked about term in all workplaces, as well as in the modern world we live in. In this final chapter, I will discuss why it's an overlooked but critical life skill. The word intelligence is rarely linked with emotions. We often use this word to define someone's academic ability or the extent of their knowledge about a variety of subjects.

> A definition of emotional intelligence is: *"The ability to identify emotions in yourself and in others, and to use this ability to manage your relationships with those around you."*

As mentioned in chapter 9, the British education system, and its obsession with GCSEs, A Levels and other nationally accredited qualifications, seems to have only one way to define intelligence. This is interesting, because during my time working at a professional football club and at schools and universities, I worked with several coaches and/or teaching assistants who hadn't acquired these formal higher level qualifications, but were ironically more skilled than many of their traditionally more qualified colleagues higher up the chain.

Regrettably in sport, however, it is rare for coaches to discuss these attributes with an athlete and use terms such as emotional intelligence. Their obsession with 'time on the grass' often masks the importance of these conversations. I was privileged to work with the England U15 football team squad selection process. In August 2017, I was involved in a three-week camp that was magnificent. Using classroom-based workshops to discuss technical and tactical strategies is good practice, but utilising the time in the day to include psychological support and group cohesion tasks was first class. Often in elite sport, these processes of development are looked upon as merely an add-on to an athlete's training programme. In contrast, maybe they are one of the main methods that bring success for many athletes and teams? The traditional opinion which many still believe, is that only ABILITY and 'on-the-field learning' is the key to becoming successful, but the trained eye knows that training on the grass just in isolation is not effective. The question is, therefore:

Is ability or talent on its own enough to make a team successful?

I think everyone has different opinions on this, but ask any expert and they will give the same answer… NO! As I mentioned previously, talent will never be enough. In metaphorical terms, it may buy you a ticket for the aeroplane, but it won't help you get the round the world trip you desire. I have seen thousands of 'talented' athletes who are unable to manage various aspects of their off-the-field behaviour, or control their off the field life to help them succeed on the pitch. They end up falling short because of this lack of understanding regarding who they truly are.

> *A saying I learnt many years ago was this,*
> *"Everybody knows more than somebody."*

So, with this in mind, relationships that are built between athletes and those who can offer them help and support are a vital component to long-term success. The coach/athlete relationship is key. Now, as an example, let's link the aforementioned saying to team sports and a major tournament, such as a football world cup. We all know about the talents and skills of Messi and Ronaldo, and the passing patterns and world-renowned techniques of the Spanish team, but:

- Would a team be more successful if the quotes about emotional intelligence and the power of the group were implemented and players and staff enjoyed greater personal bonds and unity?

In contrast:

> - Would a business thrive and achieve greater performance outcomes if the earlier definitions were also adhered to?

I think we all know the answer.

In my experience, institutional change (football club, rugby club, business or school), as well as productivity and success rates, will only be achieved if the emotional intelligence of the staff regularly contributes to enhancing morale, cohesion and harmony, with selfless acts taking place day after day. In sporting terms, this would also include the players. Years of research has proven that the more this type of behaviour is displayed in your teams or work environment, the more you will all succeed, which supports the term 'we, not me'.

The balance between this selfless, off-the-field mentality, compared with the actual performance-orientated processes that make you a great teacher, coach, teammate or boss, is paramount. After all, if everyone was kind and selfless all day in elite performance environments, but clueless about how to get results at work or win matches, then the emotional intelligence process would be a flawed strategy anyway. As an example, there would be no point in having a load of polite and caring international cricket players if none of them could bat, bowl and win matches.

You have to have the expert coaches and players in the building first. Creating a dynamic and vibrant culture should be the next step. Now, think about how you could introduce this process into your coaching, training, managing, playing and teaching methods. In the following section, I have devised a list of what I consider are the signs of having high levels of emotional intelligence. Perhaps some of them already apply to you, or maybe they don't. If this is the case and you would like to be a better coach, player, colleague, listener or expert in your field of work, then here's how to do it:

1. You have self-confidence.
   - You are in tune with your strengths and weaknesses, and you

know how to use them effectively. Most importantly, you're not afraid to admit that you're wrong or incapable of doing something. You are at ease with asking for someone else's help or advice and you never let your ego take over.

2. You know how your feelings operate.
   - You have a heightened sense of self-awareness, so you're good at examining yourself to determine exactly how you're feeling, and, more importantly, what exactly is making you feel that way.

3. You politely challenge people if you have problems with them.
   - You don't let negative moods overwhelm you and you never unprofessionally go off at people. You know this doesn't work!

   Instead, if you're upset with someone, you portray your feelings calmly and securely and let that person know exactly what's unsettling you. That way, you can solve the problem quickly and efficiently and, most importantly, calmly.

4. You're calm under pressure.
   - People look to you for reassurance when things go wrong because you don't stress. You are the go-to person when things aren't right. You're the solution finder, not the problem creator!

5. You never give up.
   - You are naturally self-motivated, which means you are the driving force behind your desire and enthusiasm for success. Because of this, you don't let small failures discourage you from pursuing the team's ultimate goals.

6. You understand other viewpoints.
   - You're able to look outside of your own life experience. You understand that the perspectives and circumstances of others are different to yours, and that this is OK and often healthy. This allows you to relate to people on multiple levels and communicate in ways you know everyone will understand.

7. You listen.
   - You value the opinions and views of all, so you take your time when you listen to them. Even more so, you ensure that you understand everything they tell you and you never interrupt them or try to manipulate or control the conversation. This makes people more willing to open up to you in the short, medium and long-term.
8. You're emotionally empathetic.
   - You're accurate at reading people's feelings, and because of this you're able to understand how they will respond. This helps you meet their needs better. You know when it's a good idea to bring something up and when it's better to just keep quiet.
9. You communicate well.
   - You articulate your thoughts in a simple, concise way, so that people know exactly what you're talking about and what you want from them. Because of the simplicity and clarity with which you explain yourself, people are eager to listen to you and not disappoint.
10. People around you feel calm.
    - You work well in groups because you are clever at making your peers feel relaxed. People feel comfortable joking and laughing around you, and you have the ability to laugh at yourself. This final point is vital, as it's a key characteristic of a successful leader.

I hope you enjoyed these reminders and, most importantly, believe that you can get your athletes to achieve these traits.

After all, sustained success is a built-in process and definitely not fluke or luck!

CONCLUSION

So, you've reached the end of my book! I feel that I have covered nearly every topic around elite performance, with the exception of nutrition advice which I know sod all about.

The chapters have mainly been short and sweet, with key messages embedded within every chapter. Hopefully, I have touched your hearts and minds. You see, holistic development is talked about everywhere, but it's never really implemented. Coaches around the world still lack the mental skills to take a step back from the technical aspects of what they are trying to achieve with the people they serve. Simply talking about football or the sport you work in isn't enough to achieve the best for the people you work with. So the book is here to help you to understand that unless you are truly holistic as a developer, you will never achieve the success you want for you or your athletes. I want you to grasp life as well as sport, because unless the two are working in tandem, sustained success will never be achieved.

I hope you've learnt and understood the following key principles:

> Behaviour for learning and people

You need to understand this process to a greater level and grasp how good behaviours enhance and accelerate learning and how bad ones hinder it. Whether you choose to call it educational psychology, social psychology, sport psychology or just knowledge, the more you know about the behaviours of people, the more you can help them. Teaching in schools for two decades has made me understand far more about both human behaviour and life than football or reading a journal ever will. Your understanding of people and not football is paramount. I have mentioned psychology processes, concepts and opinions. It doesn't take a rocket scientist to understand that England's 2018 World Cup success was driven by a culture of learning and self-improvement, and not just centred around what happened on the pitch. You need to consider the journey each individual is on more than you already do. Everyone is on a path and in order to be the best of the best, you must try to understand their journey and *their why* for playing before you understand your why for coaching. Start zooming out.

> **Subject knowledge**

You need to know your subject, whether that's football, basketball or any other sport. You need to teach them the stuff they don't already know. After all, that's the purpose of education.

> **Understand teaching and learning**

If you want to be the best coach, you need a greater understanding of the learning process in general, and in more depth. Understand that learning is different for everyone and has meaning and feelings associated with it for all athletes. Learn what effective teaching is on a deeper level. Look into your questioning techniques and your rewards and sanctions processes. Think about your motivational tools, learning climate, assessment for learning methodology, behaviour for learning concepts, differentiation, inclusion procedures, and how you strive to accelerate the learning of your athletes and help them maximise their qualities.

> **Get to grips with elite culture**

Look at how you embed elite culture into your programme and teams. Remember that culture isn't born; it is made, created, challenged, tweaked and nurtured. Please also remember that culture is only effective when your weakest athlete feels positive, cared for, nurtured and valued. Those substitutes in your squad need to feel as motivated as the captain does. After all, influencing a high-achieving athlete is the easy part. Additionally, ensure that you don't use bad facilities and resources as an excuse for poor culture or assume that exceptional ones will create a great one. It just does not work like that.

CONCLUSION

› **Mindset development**

Next in line is the mindset development of your players and, most importantly, your own. In your teaching and coaching methodology, use language like "we, not me" and instruct athletes to embrace challenge, difficulty and failure as normal. Your athletes should be able to respectfully challenge you and embrace independence as the norm. Upskill your own growth mindset so you are constantly looking to improve yourself, but avoid having your athletes see you as a know-it-all. Ensure that your language develops so that it is cleaner, clearer and more coherent for your respective cohorts.

› **Parenting and support**

The influence of parents can make or break an athlete's success. Mums and dads need to understand that their primary role is to parent their child, and it's not to be their football coach. The latter can often cause confusion for children, as they don't know whom to believe. They often won't want to let down their parents or coach by being honest about how they feel. So, if you're a parent reading this, stick to parenting and let the coach do their job. And if you're a coach reading this with difficult parents to manage, set your stall out early, create parental behaviour contracts and, if that doesn't work, tell the parents they are no longer welcome or should do the coaching themselves. That will filter them out pretty quickly. Positive support for athletes is a no brainer. Negative support ends careers before they have begun.

› **Soft skills**

In order to be the best, you need to adopt soft skills and implement them in your daily practice. As I have said many times in this book, self-awareness is the key driver to your success. Many people in football and life do not have it. They talk about themselves, think about themselves, promote themselves and get angry with themselves, and this affects others around them. That's OK if the person in question has done some walking in life and achieved a level of success, but I have never known an industry like it, where people talk a good game but do not deliver and never have. Your professional skillset is irrelevant if you have failed to grasp your personal skillset and comprehended how being kind, caring and thoughtful about other people's thoughts, feelings, emotions and opinions is a key ingredient to achieving success in life and football.

So, that's it. I've given you *all* the advice you need to be the best you can. Now it's up to you to go out there and implement it. If you understand who you truly are, how others perceive you, how you act and how you interact, you will achieve 20/20 vision going forward. Always come from a place of understanding, as this will facilitate you to react to scenarios in a way that will allow you to make the most of your ability.

Now, go and make it happen and find a solution to every problem.

Think growth not fixed, and imbue that philosophy in your teaching.

ABOUT THE AUTHOR

Steve's experiences have all been different, and he appreciates that they are unique. But they have moulded him to believe that anything is possible in terms of human change. He's witnessed 12 year olds start school wearing stab vests while heavily involved in gang culture, only to leave seven years later with a top place at university. This wasn't just one pupil, but hundreds of them. He is lucky really. He's taught 30,000 children and watched them grow into adults, so he gets to see what they have achieved at the end of their schooling.

He is now privileged to be a consultant for the England U15s national team. After his release from Brighton and Hove Albion in 1996, which was also the year he started university, he would be the first to say that if you had told him that he would be working for his national football team one day, he would have laughed. It has certainly been a journey. There's been anxiety, tears and stress – he's had it all. But, whatever happens at the Football Association, he will honestly say it was and will always be an honour to help support and represent young men and women on their way to achieving greatness.

Education and sport has been his life's passion. He says sport and not football because he is simply a lover of sport. He had tennis lessons at four and squash lessons at 10. He went on to represent Sussex at tennis in his teenage years. He is also in love with golf these days and will die a happy golfer, as he has achieved a one under par round in his lifetime, and has also hit four birdies in four consecutive holes. But he is also fully aware, however, that these two moments will never happen again off a handicap of 10.

When life as an academy footballer ended, it led him to a career in education. In 2008, Steve was shortlisted for The National Teacher of the Year Award. He has been an assistant headteacher in two large London secondary schools, with responsibility for whole-school teaching and learning, which mainly involved coaching colleagues and adding value to teaching pedagogy across several faculties. In 2006, he qualified as an advanced skills teacher and specialised in the elite delivery of physical education and behaviour for learning strategies. During this process, he helped support the labour government by providing behaviour advice for schools.

Mentoring and coaching hundreds of teachers in his career has been a passion, and he's raised attainment through effective teaching and learning strategies. This led to him being headhunted to lecture Physical Education at the University of East London between 2009 and 2012. He has lectured across the country for over a decade, including at the Institute of Education. Steve was able to pass on his knowledge about educational psychology and behaviour for learning strategies to trainee teachers. This was heavily focused on the unique balance between rewards and sanctions. School improvement has been significant to his work throughout his career in education. He's taught at two schools in special measures that were deemed successes and graded as good within two and three years, respectively. In 2013, he completed his MA in Teaching, Learning, Leadership and Psychology at King's College.

For four years, Steve was part of a highly successful Academy Management Team at Millwall Football Club, which saw 13 debuts from the academy into the first team. He is now the founder of www.solutionsmindset.com and works within the professional football and golf industries. Steve is heavily involved in ensuring that the people he works with fulfil their personal and professional objectives. This includes mental conditioning and life coaching for elite athletes, schools and business leaders. He leads discussions with players and staff about how to improve levels of self-awareness with regards to the reflective process, and he also supports them to achieve outstanding outcomes in every facet of their role, through both applied and theoretical methodologies.

You can connect with him at ss@solutionsmindset.com.

ACKNOWLEDGEMENTS

I need to thank all the people who have helped me along the way throughout my life. But really my stalwarts are my mum, Dee, dad, Tom, step mum, Jane, my sisters, Harry and Emma, and my brother, Iain. I'd also like to thank my Auntie Sheila, Uncle David, Jamie and godmother Sue for their time and effort with me. To godfather Pete, Teddy and Phil for giving me more father figures than I could have possibly have imagined. And of course Sidney Sallis my grandad still going strong at 95 years old.

Without these people, I am half the man. For a lad that failed all his GCSEs, I haven't done too badly. My brother, a former PE teacher and now a school principal, has been a massive influence in my life and is also my best friend. He has always stood by me. To be honest, the fact that his mates were three years older and regularly beat me up and smacked me around the back of the head in school corridors is probably what helped build my resilience early in life.

Thank you to my front cover models. Brad Collins of Chelsea FC, Ebere Eze of QPR FC, Marcel Staines and his mother Anna and finally to my photogragher, Tony Gameiro for being a thoroughly top bloke. Veronica of Millwall, what a lady you are. You make things happen so seamlessly and Alexa Whitten from The Book Refinery, who helped me get my book published.

Thanks to players agencies, Dirk Hebel Sports Consultancy, New Era Global Sports, and player care company Phoenix Sports Management for their trust with their players and businesses. All diligent professionals.

My thanks to Dave Hunt and Doron Salomon at the fabulous CAA Base for their wonderful support and belief in my work. Gary Petit CEO of Integral Sports Management for his constant loyalty. Ebere Eze of Crystal Palace Fc, and Brad Collins of Barnsley Fc. Also Thanks to Robbo at AFC Wimbledon and Russell Martin of MK Dons who I regard as proper Leaders. Both...Official People Carriers! Brilliant men.

My thanks, madly, truly and deeply, also go to my university crew, who have been brothers and sisters to me. They are: Wheelo, Wilky, Terry, Mallin, Rose, Powelly Boy, Shadow, Surry, Leckie. Additional thanks to Razor, Pottsy, Kitkat, Spawny, Bally, Dennis, Gibbsy, OB, Bomber and Big Russ. My thanks also to: Phill H, Harry and Larry, and, of course, Livers. You have seen me at my best and worst and are my extended family.

To my Brighton crew – Charman, Megan, Whitey, Mozza, Peters, Barton, Owen, Lovett, Smithy, Dinesy, Enty, Berry, Wattsy and Kevin – for 35 years of friendship. I'd also like to mention my golfing friends from the GLB – what people you are and what friends you have become. There have been so many laughs.

My thanks to former pupil Chris Eather for changing my life. Tom and Gav from League Football Education for showing the loyalty when it mattered. To Joe from Charlton Athletic and Karen G. To Popey for being my token rugby friend, and to Shrooty and Danny Lee for challenging me and making me better.

Finally to the Millwall staff, players and parents, who stood by me through my moans and groans for four long and gruelling seasons. To the players that have now become friends all over the world. You know who you are: top people, top club and top professionals. I care about that club, I really do.

Printed in Great Britain
by Amazon

43690964R00155